SMOKE, WOOD, FIRE

SMOKE, WOOD, FIRE

The **ADVANCED GUIDE**
to **SMOKING MEAT**

Jeff Phillips

whitecap

DESIGN Andrew Bagatella and Setareh Ashrafologhalai
PHOTOGRAPHY BY John Edward O'Connor, Miller Photography, Tulsa, OK; and courtesy of the author.

Library and Archives Canada Cataloguing in Publication

Title: Smoke, wood, fire : the advanced guide to smoking meat/Jeff Phillips.
Names: Phillips, Jeff, 1970- author.
Description: Includes index.
Identifiers: Canadiana 20190208392 | ISBN 9781770503267 (softcover)
Subjects: LCSH: Smoked meat. | LCSH: Smoking (Cooking) | LCSH: Cooking (Meat) | LCSH: Smoking of
    food—Handbooks, manuals, etc. | LCSH: Meat—Preservation—Handbooks, manuals, etc.
Classification: LCC TX609 .P45 2020 | DDC 641.4/9—dc23

We acknowledge the financial support of the Government of Canada through the Canada Book Fund (CBF) for our publishing activities and the Province of British Columbia through the Book Publishing Tax Credit.

Nous reconnaissons l'appui financier du gouvernement du Canada et la province de la Colombie-Britannique par le Book Publishing Tax Credit.

Printed in Hong Kong by Sheck Wah Tong

7 6 5 4 3 2 1

I would like to dedicate this book to my sweetheart, girlfriend and lifelong companion, on this, our 25th year of marriage. She has been so patient with me as I worked on these pages into the wee hours of the morning at times. Her constant encouragement and willingness to help with whatever I need is more than I could ever ask for. Please know that some part of the proceeds from this book will go toward taking this girl somewhere really special because she deserves it!

FOREWORD

BACK IN 2009 I received an email from a subscriber of mine who happened to be an editor of a prominent publishing company. He wanted to know if I'd like to write a book on smoking meat. He explained that this would be distributed and sold in brick and mortar bookstores as well as online, would take 8-10 months to produce once they had my final draft and, while it would be a lot of work, it would also be worth it.

I don't know if I really understood what I was getting into but it seemed like an exciting venture and a logical next step on my popular website *smoking-meat.com*. So, after thinking about it for an entire five minutes (and then waiting a day or two to respond as to not sound too eager), I said "yes."

That first book–*Smoking Meat: The Essential Guide to Real Barbecue*–was a lot of work—long, hard grueling hours at my desk pecking away at the keyboard, researching, cooking, running out to the shed to check something on a particular smoker or to snap a photo.

I quickly discovered that writing a cookbook was not for the lazy or the weak! I was missing dinner way too often, staying at home working while the rest of the family was out having fun. I caught myself declining a lot of invitations explaining that I had to "work on the book." I am quite certain that my friends and family got really tired of me saying that!

After about three months of editing the copy was deemed finished and the manuscript worthy of design.

Many of the recipes were prepared and the glamorous food shots were taken, which made me look a lot more professional than I really am. Folks, if you know a great food photographer and food stylist, give them a hug because they deserve that and more. They can make you look that good. Mine sure did!

The book was printed and the sales started to roll in. From day one *Smoking Meat* has been an absolute success, and it never stops amazing me how many are still sold each and every week.

For the last two or three years I guess I knew it was inevitable that I would produce a second book–but procrastination seemed to win most days. Hey, I produce a fresh newsletter recipe every week, review new products, answer hundreds of emails, and maintain all my social media–not to mention, I have a life!

But alas, the time came and I finally committed to book #2. And I knew, way back deep in my brain, that I wanted to knock this one out of the park, too. The first book covered smoking basics with lots of recipes. But with *Smoke Wood Fire*, I want to take you to the next level.

In this book, I will cover a wide selection of tools, equipment, and smoking supplies including various types and brands of smokers, slicers and dehydrators, thermometers, injectors and even things like mops, brushes, and heat-safe gloves and mitts just to mention a few. We'll also delve into the various types of wood, charcoal and other fuel that you'll use in your smoker and how to use them to obtain the best results.

In addition to equipment, I will go over all of the techniques that will help you hone this craft in your path to becoming the best pitmaster you can be. Through research, making mistakes and sometimes just getting lucky, I have been perfecting these techniques for more than twenty-five years and I am passionate about sharing what I have learned with you.

Some of the techniques and methods you will find in this book include brining, smoke production, cooking outdoors in cold climates, cooking at high altitudes, temperature control–and there's even a complete how-to on curing and smoking

your own bacon with plenty of full-color pictures to guide you along and make sure it ends up perfect.

I have poured my love for outdoor cooking and years of knowledge into this book in a way that is easy to read and simple to understand. With your passion and desire to learn, we will make great things happen out by the smoker.

Yours in smoke, fire and amazing food cooked in your backyard!

CONTENTS

LARGE EQUIPMENT

For the most part, this section will refer to your smoker whether it's electric, pellet, charcoal, gas or even a big stick burner. There are a number of different options in this category, as you will see, and we'll go over each one in as much detail as we can so you can learn what is available and what might be the perfect unit for you and your family.

REC TEC RT-700 pellet smoker "The Bull"

THE RIGHT SMOKER

If you are just getting into smoking meat then you might be able to use your grill as a makeshift smoker for a while. But eventually, you'll want to purchase a dedicated smoker. As with everything else, purchase the very best you can afford.

Do your homework though and make sure you do plenty of research on each type of smoker to find the right one that will work best for the type of cooking that you do.

Here's a few things that will guide your decision:

WHERE YOU LIVE: If you live in an apartment, duplex or some other type of housing community, you might not be allowed to use a big offset smoker or one that produces a real fire. That said, you might be able to use a small electric smoker on your patio or balcony. Be sure and check the appropriate rules and regulations in your location before committing.

YOUR WALLET: Smokers can be found for under $100 while others can cost in the thousands and everywhere in between. Only you know your budget and this will most likely be a huge driving factor in the size and type of smoker you can purchase.

WHAT TYPE OF FOODS YOU LIKE TO COOK: If you just want to make a few appetizers now and then, you can probably get by with a small electric

Meadow Creek reverse flow wood smoker.

smoker or perhaps an upright water/bullet smoker. But if you plan on roasting the occasional pig and/or cooking ribs for your boy scout troop, you'll want to invest in a large offset smoker or perhaps a vertical propane or pellet smoker that has a lot of rack space.

FUEL: The main smoker fuels are charcoal, wood, electricity, and gas (propane or natural gas). However, not all of these may be available where you want to cook. For instance, if you want to take the smoker on primitive camping trips, then this rules out electric smokers or other smokers that use electricity, such as pellet smokers. You would probably want a lightweight bullet smoker for this and, if you need more cooking space, just get two of them. Gas could be an option but normally gas units are on the heavy side.

HOW LAZY YOU ARE: I use the term "lazy" very loosely as I think all of us have an idea of how much work we want to put into certain tasks. So the question is, How much work do you want to put into cooking outdoors? If you enjoy poking

and tending the fire for hours on end, then an offset smoker might be the right choice for you– and you can get offset smokers in all sizes. But if your idea of cooking is to get it all set up and then park yourself in a lawn chair and not really worry about it again for hours, then you'll want to look into an electric or even a pellet smoker for quick start-ups and little to no hands-on during the entire cook time.

HORIZONTAL OFFSET SMOKER

Ranging from small to very large, this type of smoker is easily identified by its larger, barrel shaped smoke chamber with a smaller firebox attached to the side, usually offset or set a little lower than the smoke chamber.

With one or more intake vents in the firebox, and a chimney attached to the smoke chamber, the unit is able to draw air into the firebox and then into the smoke chamber, across the meat and exiting via the chimney which pulls the smoke along with it.

In many of these horizontal offset smokers the heat and smoke travel from the firebox directly

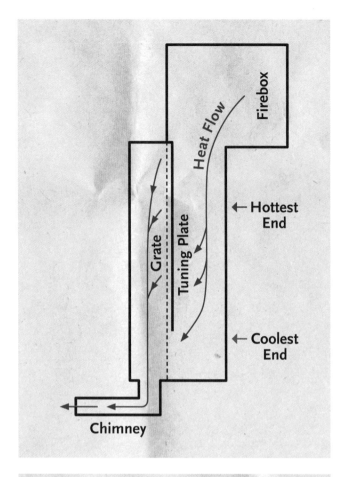

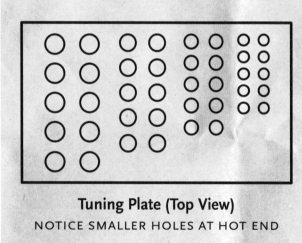

Tuning Plate (Top View)
NOTICE SMALLER HOLES AT HOT END

TOP Heat flow in a normal horizontal offset smoker.
BOTTOM Tuning plate installation in a horizontal offset.

up to the grate, across the grate to the chimney on the opposite side. This usually means the area closest to the firebox is very hot and the temperature gets gradually cooler as you move to the other side. This is not a huge problem since you can plan your cooks accordingly and place poultry or burgers on the hot end and things like ribs and brisket on the cooler side. The poultry, burgers, steaks etc. will benefit from the higher heat while the other stuff will enjoy the normal smoking temperatures.

Tuning plates are sometimes installed to help even out this inconsistent heat. To best understand a tuning plate, imagine a thick steel plate that runs under the grate with small and fewer holes on the hot end, and larger and more numerous holes toward the cooler end. This helps equalize the amount of heat that is able to get up to the grate.

Some manufacturers have created horizontal offset smokers that do not have these inconsistent heat problems due to a full metal plate that runs under the grate for the length of the smoke chamber. There are no holes or outlets until you get to the end opposite the firebox and the chimney is located on the same side as the firebox. You are probably wondering how in the heck that works . . . well, let me explain. This design is called "reverse flow" which forces the heat to travel out of the firebox, under the grate and is not allowed to come up and in contact with the food until it gets to the very end of the smoke chamber at which point, there is an opening.

Most of these smokers are rounded at the end to help the airflow make that 180 degree turn quickly, reversing the flow, so it can move across the top of the grate, kissing the meat gently and evenly just before it exits out via the chimney.

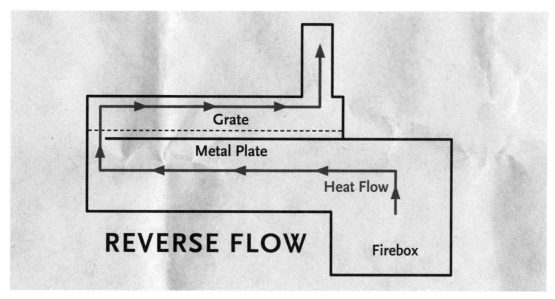

Heat flow in a normal horizontal offset smoker.

While we call most of these smokers "wood-burners" or "stickburners," I highly recommend using lump charcoal as the main heat source for these, even the really large ones, and then adding wood, a stick or two at a time, to provide the smoke. This is the set-up and method you'll see on the competition trail and among many professionals.

One alternative to using charcoal is to load the firebox with sticks or splits of wood which you then turn into heat-producing coals. Often a propane weed-burner is employed for this job, and it works quite well I might add, although it can be a little time consuming. I'll advise, though, that you leave all the vents and the smoke chamber lid or door open during the initial process of burning the wood down to coals as it produces lots of dirty smoke and you want this stuff to exit quickly rather than settle onto the grates and walls of the smoker.

Another option would be to burn wood down to coals in a separate barrel or even a pit in the ground and then shovel the coals into the firebox

as needed to maintain the goal temperature.

As with all things, practice makes perfect and you will soon learn all the nuances of your particular unit and what makes it cook at exactly the temperature you want with just the perfect amount of smoke flavor.

I have a Meadowcreek TS120P which is a wood burning smoker made from a 120-gallon tank. It's quite large but designed to be pushed around the patio on its wheels rather than being mounted on a trailer like many of the other large wood burning units.

WATER/BULLET SMOKERS

I first started using water smokers years ago and nearly everything I learned about controlling the temperature, keeping the meat moist via the use of the water pan, how much wood to use for the proper smoke flavor, and even how to plan ahead and time the meat to get it done at the right time was learned and practiced to perfection on this cheap, box-store smoker.

LEFT Masterbuilt Charcoal Bullet Smoker   **RIGHT** Top of the Weber Smoky Mountain removed.

I have always said that if you can learn how to smoke on one of these cheap, hard-to-use charcoal bullet smokers, you can probably cook on anything. It's like bootcamp for smoking meat.

I often recommend that newbies start out on one of these more difficult smokers if you are really serious about learning the art of smoking meat—even though there are much easier options available.

Let's talk about that el cheapo smoker that so many of us started out on. Many were made by Brinkmann and could be found at various big-box stores or online at Amazon. These have become known as El Cheapo Brinkmanns or an ECB.

This smoker consisted of a barrel and a lid, a few brackets with mounting hardware to hold the water pan and the charcoal pan in place, and of course the infamous gauge on the top which didn't give you the temperature but rather, three

really helpful tips on how the heat was doing consisting of warm, ideal, and hot.

Oh, and let's not forget the three spindly legs that held the smoker up off the ground.

To get it started you simply made up a batch of lit charcoal using a charcoal chimney (see page 120) and poured it into the charcoal pan, placed the water pan on top of that, then lowered the grate and then the upper grate into place.

A small door on the side allowed you to add woodchips and more charcoal as needed to keep the heat at some sort of respectable level such as "ideal."

The lid did not fit well and this allowed too much air to get into the coals making it difficult to control. I pushed pieces of foil down between the lid and the body of the smoker to seal it up a little better. With a little trial and error, this helped it work a lot better but it still did not work great.

To better control heat and smoke, I glued felt strips (made for the Big Green Egg) around the door opening.

Main components of the Weber Smoky Mountain.

I later realized that it was not getting enough air to the charcoal pan and as if this was not bad enough, after a few hours, the ashes from the burnt charcoal had nowhere to go and would snuff out the lit coals.

A few holes drilled in the bottom of the charcoal pan and a really small grate held the charcoal up off the bottom turning this humdrum smoker into a much more precise machine.

I have smoked more than my share of ribs, brisket, chicken, you name it, on this smoker before and after my engineered adjustments and those were some good times, baby!

You can still find these smokers, sometimes under different brand names with slightly different designs, but they all work pretty much in the same way and many of the adjustments that were made on these still work on the newer versions if you care to go old school.

Bullet smokers, though, aren't all cheap and they aren't all difficult to use. Let's discuss the Weber Smoky Mountain, dubbed the "WSM" by its huge cult following.

The WSM is designed and built for heat control and while it's not perfect, it comes about as close as you're going to get using charcoal for fuel and trying to maintain a consistent temperature over multiple hours of cook time.

The overall pill shape of the smoker with the dome top, inverted dome on the bottom and, of course, the four vents that allow you to adjust the airflow down to the most precise amount, are all part of what makes this smoker work so well.

One of the vents is located on the top where the smoke exits while the other three, located around the bottom of the smoker, let you adjust the intake of air to the charcoal.

Inside the smoker you'll find a grate and ring to hold the charcoal close to the bottom of the

TOP
The original thermometer on the old ECB.

MIDDLE
The one and only El Cheapo Brinkmann (ECB).

BOTTOM
Drilled holes in the ECB charcoal pan to increase airflow to the charcoal.

smoker, a large water pan just above that, and then a lower grate and upper grate to give you fairly ample space for cooking.

The lid houses the exit vent and the factory-installed thermometer.

If this smoker has a flaw, it's in the access panel on the side which doesn't always fit flush to the body of the smoker thereby letting uncontrolled air into the smoker. If you are careful, you can adjust the curvature of this door to make it fit flush.

Another option is to apply some heat-resistant felt to the area around the door using heat-resistant glue or epoxy. I did this to mine several years ago and it worked really well.

I must warn you that anytime you modify your smoker by either drilling holes, applying glue, etc, it will most likely void any warranty you might have so go into such projects with this in mind.

There are two or three really cool ways to set up the charcoal in this type of smoker to give you hours of perfect, low and slow heat. I will discuss this later beginning on page 125.

KETTLE GRILLS

Kettles are not really smokers but they are super easy to set-up as a smoker with indirect cooking. That's why they are included in this list and for that reason alone.

There's a whole slew of companies that make kettles but the one I am most familiar with and see most often is the one made by Weber, a brand we all know very well. They've been in business for years and do a superb job of marketing their products. When you think of grilling, you just sort of think of a Weber kettle grill in the back-yard (or at least I do).

The basic kettle has a shallow "kettle" shaped pan sitting on three legs. As you go up in price

you get extra features like wheels, an ash catcher under the pan so you don't catch your deck on fire, and some even have a handle you can slide back and forth to stir the ashes which allow them to fall through to the pan below.

To light this thing up, simply pour a healthy amount of charcoal into the pan, douse it with the flammable substance of your choice, and light 'er up! This brings back somewhat fond memories from childhood, seeing the menfolk pouring everything from kerosene to gasoline and rubbing alcohol on the charcoal as a makeshift lighter fluid during family barbecues. They'd always yell "look out" just as they struck the match and threw it onto the mound of charcoal. I shudder now when I think about it but back then, as a boy, it was pretty exciting seeing that fire leap twenty feet into the

Weber Original Kettle 22-inch charcoal grill

2-zone set-up in a Weber Kettle.

air and nearly catch the eaves of the house on fire.

But I digress.

So to use one of these kettles as an indirect low-and-slow smoker you do what is called "setting-up zones" by piling all of the hot charcoal to one side. The meat is placed on the grate over the area without charcoal. In this way you have a hot side and a cool side known as a two-zone fire. You can get crazy with it and create three zones as well by placing a lot of charcoal over about a third of the area, a lot less charcoal in another third, and then an area with no charcoal at all.

To really take it to true indirect cooking though, you need to place a water pan under the grate on the side that has no charcoal. The water heats up, creates steam and helps to stabilize the heat. The humidity also goes up inside the cooking area which is great for getting moister food at the end by decreasing the natural drying effect of heat.

There is the Smokenator which I cover on page 95, but suffice it to say, this contraption makes it easy to keep the charcoal on one side of the charcoal pan, together with a water pan to add a little humidity, and at the same time leaves most of the grill grate area open for cooking with indirect heat. Place woodchips or chunks over the coals as needed and you are truly smoking.

KAMADO COOKERS

Kamado cookers, also called ceramic cookers, are often made of a thick ceramic material which retains heat really well. Some of the newer, less expensive kamado cookers are made of double or triple wall steel with heavy insulation for that high fuel efficiency that is expected from this type of grill.

Some cookers of this type are Big Green Egg (BGE), Primo, Grill Dome, Kamado Joe, Grilla Kong and the Akorn by Char-griller.

Komodo Kamado

Char-Griller Akorn

Big Green Egg

All of these are styled after the clay cooking vessels found in Asian archeology sites dating back more than 3,000 years ago. The thick walls help to not only insulate the inside and hold in the heat but the walls themselves heat up like a firebrick, storing the heat and releasing it very efficiently over a long period of time.

When I open the lid on my Big Green Egg, the temperature often drops momentarily but it recovers very quickly just as soon as I close it. This is due to that stored heat in the walls of the unit.

A kamado cooker is usually egg shaped and may or may not have a base or legs that hold it up. Inside you will find an area in the bottom for charcoal, usually a plate to shield the food from the heat so you can cook indirectly, and a cooking grate above that. In the BGE, this plate is called a "plate setter."

There are vents in the bottom to control the air to the charcoal and a vent or lid in the top to allow the heat and/or smoke to exit. A thermometer in the lid will allow you to monitor the temperature although I have found that these are not as accurate as one placed at grate level where the food is located.

The Big Green Egg and some other cookers of this type have an opening at the bottom for raking out the ashes. The charcoal burns very efficiently so ashes collect rather slowly. I usually rake out the ashes after several cooks and, about once or twice a year depending on how often I use it, the unit is taken completely apart, vacuumed out, air holes cleared and put back together. During this cleaning I also like to oil the springs and hardware in the lid to make sure everything is in tip top-shape.

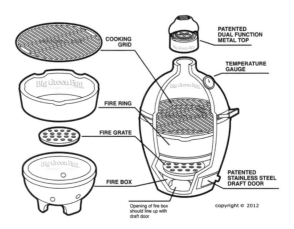

Kamado cooker breakdown.

Primo Oval

Kamado Joe

Each of these kamado cookers will have its own set of instructions for setting up the charcoal and how to place the woodchips and/or chunks for the best smoke production.

In the Big Green Egg, I use lump charcoal and fill the charcoal basin up to the air holes.

To light the BGE, I like to bury two or three paraffin fire starters down in the center of the charcoal.

Once the fire starters are lit, I put some large pieces of charcoal over and around the center. Within about seven minutes, I have a nice glowing area of heat right in the center which is about six inches in diameter. This is about the right amount for heating the BGE to normal smoking temperatures of 225-240°F.

This is the time to sprinkle some woodchips over the top of the charcoal in a spiral design or you can place a metal box full of woodchips just off center to give you several hours of thin smoke.

I also sometimes place a small split of wood just off center so it gets enough heat to make it smoke but not enough to catch fire.

With the smoke wood in place, insert the plate setter or whatever it's called on your kamado cooker, set the cooking grate in place, and close the lid.

Make sure the bottom and top vents are full open until the temperature gets within about 30-40°F of your set temperature. At that point, begin closing the top and bottom vents as much as needed to keep the temperature to just below your set temperature.

Remember you can always bring the temperature up by giving it a little more air but it's very difficult to bring it back down on this type of cooker.

Once the temperature is where you want it, it's time to cook.

Kamado cookers will allow you to cook for hours on end with only very small adjustments here and there and using minimal charcoal.

A word of caution: It is important to "burp" kamado cookers when opening them during the cooking session. The sudden influx of air can cause a flare-up so you do not want to open the lid all the way at once. The trick is to open it just a few inches at first, wait a few seconds, and then you can open it all the way. Remembering this can save you from a sudden and unexpected blast of heat and flames.

Big Green Egg XL

Raising the heavy lid is made easy due to a special hinge.

The thick ceramic walls and the gasket around the cooking area
help to retain heat so it can recover quickly after the lid is open.

DRUM/BARREL SMOKERS

Backyard barbecuers have been making grills, smokers, and cookers out of metal trashcans and drums for several decades at least and possibly longer than that. I started hearing the name "Ugly Drum Smoker" (UDS) back in the early 2000's. This name was given to smokers that were constructed using a metal barrel or drum that was burned out to make it safe for use. Hardware and pipe fittings were incorporated to give it vents in the bottom and top, a charcoal area in the bottom which often included a basket with one or more cooking grates, and of course the lid which was used to close off the cooker so the air could be controlled with the vents.

Since that time, some people started manufacturing these drum smokers and selling them to the public at a very affordable price. One such company is Pit Barrel Cookers (PBC). One of the things that they really honed in on was the hanging of the meat instead of laying it on a grate.

This was not a new concept but it was not well known. PBC sends their barrels with two pieces of rebar that fit through special holes in the side of the barrel and several meat hooks. The hooks go through the meat and hang on the rebar over the fire allowing the juices to run down over the meat and drip onto the fire while it cooks, enhancing the flavor even more. As such, there is a huge cult following of PBC owners that are now hanging and cooking meat simply because this method was brought to market in such an ingenious way.

Another such company which manufactures drum smokers is Barrel House Cookers (BHC) which follows a similar hanging system concept to suspend meat such as ribs, chicken, even brisket over the fire.

The ugly drum smokers were being built by DIY backyard barbecuers who wanted an inexpensive way to build a smoker using supplies, tools, and equipment that were fairly easy to

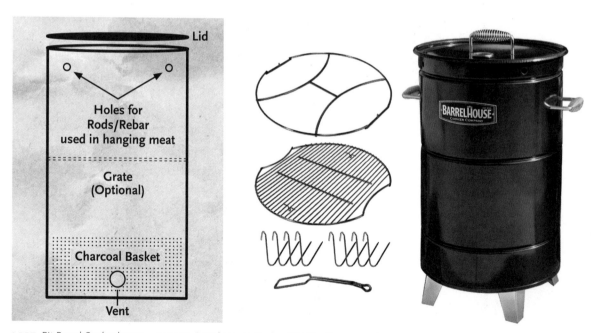

LEFT Pit Barrel Cooker layout. **RIGHT** Barrel House Cooker (BHC) with accessories.

Parallel bars on this
drum cooker allow you to
suspend meat on hooks
over the charcoal.

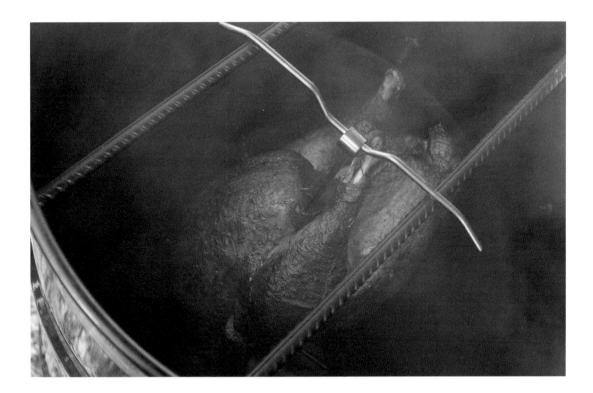

obtain. But everyone doesn't have the time or the know-how to build an ugly drum smoker so this created a need ready to be filled.

The premise behind the UDS is that if you can control the airflow into and out of the smoker, you can very precisely control the temperature for hours on end using small amounts of charcoal.

Unlike the kamado cookers, the drums are not thick walled and aren't made of a heat storing material like ceramic. But because they are air tight (except for the bottom and top vents), they are very fuel efficient and can be set up to cook for many hours with only minimal adjustments.

Manufacturers of these drum smokers often recommend briquettes instead of lump charcoal for better heat control, but many drum smoker owners successfully use lump charcoal. Find out about the differences between these two types of charcoal on page 118.

To set up a drum smoker for cooking, load charcoal into the charcoal pan or basket. Usually a preset amount of unlit charcoal and then a preset amount of already lit charcoal is placed on top.

This is called the "Minion method" of cooking and is discussed in depth starting on page 127.

If you are confused about how to get pre-lit charcoal, you'll need to read about the wonderful use of the charcoal chimney on page 120.

The cooking grate(s) are put into place, the lid is closed and the vents are adjusted to bring the temperature up to your desired cooking level. Manufactured units will tell you exactly where to set the bottom vent based on your elevation range for easy start-up, but this is not to say that the vents can't be adjusted a little to your own preferences. Recommended settings on the PBC based on your elevation are found on the following graph.

Woodchips are usually dropped from the cooking grate down to the charcoal below to create smoke but you can also mix chunks of wood into the charcoal to give you continuous and consistent wood smoke throughout the cooking process.

Drum smokers often hold temperatures that are on the upper end of the smoking temperature range and for this reason, the food will get done a little quicker than in a traditional smoker.

These cookers will also come with a method to hang meat such as chicken, ribs, and even brisket providing a little different option than just laying it on a cooking grate. This vertical arrangement causes the fat and juices that render out to run down over the meat and onto the coals below, keeping the meat basted while it cooks.

Incidentally, drum smoking has a very large following which I don't think is going to die down anytime soon.

I like some of the added features on the BHC as well. First, it is designed so you can lift the entire drum up off the charcoal basket. This makes it easier than the PBC to add more charcoal or smoking wood mid-cook if you need to.

The BHC also has a bracket on the back side of the lid that makes it easy to hang it on the side of the barrel while you are tending the food, moving the grates, what have you.

The PBC is also a really good barrel smoker. I love the horseshoe handle on the lid and, of course, using rebar to hang the meat is "off-the-hook" awesome. This smoker has a large, almost cult-like following and is one of the original manufacturers of barrel/drum smokers.

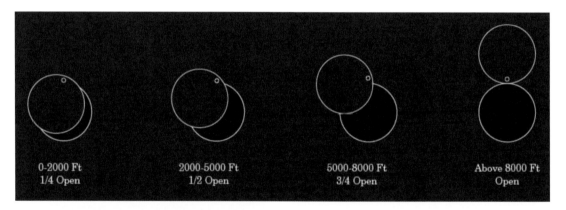

| 0-2000 Ft 1/4 Open | 2000-5000 Ft 1/2 Open | 5000-8000 Ft 3/4 Open | Above 8000 Ft Open |

ABOVE PBC vent settings.   **LEFT** Ready to hang some meat.   **RIGHT** Lit charcoal on top.

| Landmann propane (wide) | Masterbuilt propane | Charbroil propane | Landmann propane (open) | Landmann propane (closed) |

GAS SMOKERS (PROPANE)

Very early on in my smoking career I obtained a Landmann propane smoker from a local box store and that's how I very quickly fell in love with propane smokers. With propane as fuel, all you really have to do is keep the woodchip box full to obtain some of the best tasting smoked meat with the prettiest smoke rings you've ever seen.

With propane so easily accessible and so portable, this gives you the option of taking an easy-to-use smoker with you when you go camping, to the lake, or even to the park for a cookout.

Because these smokers are so easy to manage, you can simply set one up and then go do some other things that don't include babysitting the smoker–like throwing a line into the water, playing some ball or Frisbee or even taking on some short trails while the food is cooking.

Unlike electric, you can't leave it for long but you can leave it for an hour or so at a time–and with the flavor and smoke ring advantages over electric, it may just be worth it.

Propane smokers usually look like tall vertical cabinets with a full-size door that opens in the front giving you easy access to the water pan, wood chip box, and the cooking grates.

Some models give you multiple doors so you can add water or woodchips without disturbing the heat in the cooking area which is certainly a nice feature to have, in my opinion.

A burner in the bottom runs on propane and just above that is the woodchip box which can vary from a thin metal box to a large heavy cast iron box like the one that's in the wide-body Landmann that I now own.

The larger heavier woodchip box takes longer to smoke but it is more durable and seems to smoke longer once it gets going.

Above the woodchip box is a water pan which also serves as a drip pan. This water pan creates some humidity in the smoker which helps stabilize the heat and reduces the natural drying effects of heated air. The water pan also acts as a heat shield between the fire and the food giving you the indirect cooking method that you want when cooking low and slow.

My propane smoker came with four grates but this will vary from brand to brand.

There are many solid smoker manufacturers that carry propane models such as Landmann, Masterbuilt, and Charbroil.

The temperature inside a propane smoker is usually controlled by adjusting the flame up or down via a rotary "control" knob. As you use your smoker more and more, you will learn the correct flame setting that provides the heat level you want to maintain.

Pit Boss Copperhead 7 Series pellet smoker

My lighting procedure consists of placing the water pan into the smoker, turning on the propane, and then quickly using the built-in igniter button on the bottom to create a spark which lights the burner. You can also use a lighter or butane torch to light the burner.

I like to preheat the smoker for about 20 minutes before I'm ready to cook and, in most cases, the woodchips don't go in until the food does.

To set up the woodchip box, I've found that adding wood chunks first then filling in the gaps with woodchips and/or wood pellets gives me the best smoke for the longest period of time.

When I am ready to place the food in the smoker, I add the woodbox into the smoker, turn the heat to high and then after placing the food on the smoker grates, leave the door ajar so it doesn't get too hot inside the smoker.

Once I see good smoke flowing, the door is closed all the way and the heat is adjusted to maintain my set temperature.

I often find that I get really good smoke for about two hours or more and that is often enough. But if I want to continue the smoking process, I just open the door and remove the woodchip box with a pair of channel lock pliers. The ashes are poured into a metal container and water is poured on top to distinguish them.

More wood is added to the box and it is once again placed back into the smoker using the channel lock pliers.

Since the woodchip box is really hot, it's not usually necessary to adjust the heat to high and leave the door ajar like you do at the beginning. The wood will now start smoking much faster this time and it's ok at this point if it takes a few minutes.

I highly recommend having an extra tank of propane on hand at all times. There's nothing

Woodbox full of chips–Landmann propane smoker.

worse than running out of propane in the middle of a cook and having to move all that food to the oven before it cools down. As a general rule, you'll get about 25-30 hours of cooking time out of a 20-pound tank if you are cooking at 225-240°F.

ELECTRIC SMOKERS

Electric smokers are one of the easiest smokers to use and, for this reason, if you want to cook great tasting smoked food without a lot of "babysitting," then this might just be the type of smoker for you.

In some cases, you simply plug it in, turn it on, and it's ready to go. With the more fancy ones, you can dial in a temperature and even the amount of time that you want that temperature to last. In mere minutes you are off to the races and cooking great tasting smoked food in your backyard!

Of course there are several different brands and styles, but all use a heating element, much like the one that is in your home oven, to create heat. The element usually cycles on and off to maintain the set temperature.

I own several different types of these including the Smokin-it 2D and an off-brand cabinet-style

Masterbuilt electric smoker

electric smoker that looks exactly like the Masterbuilt models.

The Masterbuilt cabinet-style electric smoker is one that I see a lot and you don't have to look far to understand why. This smoker is easy to use, lets you get some sleep while you're cooking, and turns out some really mouthwatering food. As if that's not enough, it comes out of the box ready to cook in just minutes.

As you may have guessed from my description, it looks like a tall, somewhat narrow cabinet with four racks on the inside.

Depending on which model you have, it stands from 30 to 40 inches tall, is about 25 inches wide and almost 20 inches deep. Not a bad size for cooking smoked food for family and friends.

Once opened you'll see a grease pan on the floor of the smoker with the water/drip pan on the left and the heating element/woodchip box to the right.

The four grates are fitted into slots or rails that begin just above the water pan and go all the way to the top of the smoker. It's really a pretty simple set-up.

One thing you'll notice upon further inspection is a small round chute on the right side of the smoker. This allows you to add more woodchips without having to open the door of the smoker . . . Genius! Everyone knows that when you open the door of a smoker, heat is immediately lost and must be recovered–and this woodchip chute completely eliminates that problem.

The control module is at the very top of the unit. It's here where you set the temperature and how long you want to maintain it. There is also a current smoker temperature readout.

To cook in this smoker you only have to plug it in, set the appropriate temperature and the time–and the heating element kicks in and starts preheating the smoker.

I recommend letting it preheat for at least 20-30 minutes, especially if it's cold outside.

When you're ready to place the food in the smoker, first add chips via the sidechute or open the smoker door and add woodchips to the chip drawer, depending on the model of your smoker, then place the food on the cooking grate.

By opening the doors of the smoker, some of the heat will escape. This will prod the heating element to kick on, which is located just below the woodchip drawer, causing the woodchips to start smoking.

Anytime you notice that the chips are not smoking as they should, this is probably because the heating element is not cycling on often enough and you may need to open the door and release some heat to get things going again.

Many Masterbuilt owners use the A-Maze-N smoker tray to provide constant smoke instead of using the built-in woodchip box. This is for sure not a bad thing because the A-Maze-N is inexpensive and probably the best thing you can do for your Masterbuilt-type smoker.

This accessory uses pellets. When you light it, the A-Maze-N produces smoke for 8-11 hours, uninterrupted. This not only means you don't have to worry about adding woodchips during the cooking session, it also allows you to do other things while the food cooks. Sleep, go to the store, do yard work, no problem!

For greater detail on this accessory check out page 93.

The Smokin-it 2D Smoker

The Smokin-it 2D Smoker is much like the Masterbuilt and other electric smokers except it is made completely of stainless steel and is run by a fancy computer called a PID controller. This allows it to hold a temperature that is very precise and, because it is heavily insulated, it holds these precise temperatures even in very cold or hot weather.

Smokin-it electric smoker-Wifi

To set up the Smokin-it 2D, a small amount of wood, usually three to four small chunks, equivalent to about eight ounces, is added to the woodbox and the food is laid on the cooking grates while the smoker is off. Once the wood and food are in place, the door is closed and the PID controller at the top is used to power on the smoker and program a "recipe".

The controller allows you to set multiple temperature changes based on elapsed time or acquired temperature and these programs are called "recipes."

For instance, for smoking fish I could set the controller to maintain 160 degrees for 1 hour then increase the temperature to 180 degrees and hold that until the fish reaches 140 degrees or the finish temperature that you desire. Additionally, we could program it to then decrease the temperature to 140 degrees to keep it warm until you remove it from the smoker and switch off the power.

These "recipes" are very easy to program and up to six of these programs can be saved to memory for using over and over.

The Smokin-it 2D smoker is very easy to use and it is also very easy to keep clean. The grates are small and will easily fit in the dishwasher. To reduce cleanup time, I recommend lining the floor of the smoker and lid of the woodbox with heavy-duty foil. Don't forget to make a hole in the foil right where the grease drain is located in the floor so the grease can drain out into the grease pan.

BRADLEY SMOKERS

Yes, Bradley smokers get their very own section even though they are essentially an electric smoker and heated via an electric element just like those in an electric oven or stovetop.

Smokin-it 2D electric smoker made of all stainless steel and heavily insulated for heat retention.

This model comes with 4 racks which can be moved around or removed to best accommodate what you are cooking.

LEFT Bradley 4-rack digital smoker **RIGHT** Bradley Smart smoker

The distinction is in the way it creates smoke by automatically moving wooden "pucks" onto a hot plate, completely independent from the heating element.

The Bradley smoker is known far and wide– and for good reason. It is easy to use, and has that famous built-in automation that feeds pucks or bisquettes made of wood for continual smoke lasting just shy of 10 hours.

The Bradley looks like a tall narrow box or cabinet with a smoke generator attached to the bottom left side. With the generator attached, it is approximately 24 inches wide, 14 inches deep, and 31 to 39 inches high, depending on the model you purchase.

The entire front side is the door which gives excellent access to whatever you are cooking.

Inside you will find four to six racks, depending on the model, which slide in and out on rails. The racks are approximately 11 inches by 15 inches and made of chrome-plated steel.

Inside the smoker there is a heating element like in most electric smokers which controls the cooking temperature. Additionally, there is a hot plate that the wood puck sits on. The temperature of the hot plate is not adjustable but provides just the right amount of heat to cause the wood to smoke without catching fire.

As you can see, by having separate and independent controls, you can easily hot smoke or cold smoke foods on a whim.

The mechanism in the smoke generator pushes a new wood puck onto the hot plate every 20 minutes, in turn pushing the spent puck into a bowl of water.

Because of this nifty mechanism, you can set it up so you have an oven temperature and a set oven time, as well as a smoke time. You can then go to work, do chores, even go to bed knowing that the smoker has your back because there's no need to manage it further.

The newer Bradley smart smoker even allows you to set and monitor the smoker on your smart phone via bluetooth technology. Very nifty!

HASTY BAKE

The Hasty Bake is manufactured in Tulsa, OK and is well known for its crank which allows you to move the firebox up and down for low and slow smoking to hot and fast searing and everything in between.

Another great feature is the "v" shape of the cooking grates which allows grease to run to the center then drip down into a channel so it can run out to the drip pan, preventing flare-ups.

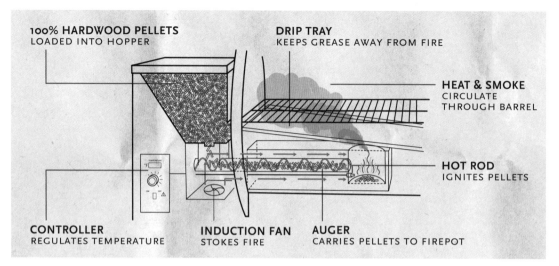

100% HARDWOOD PELLETS LOADED INTO HOPPER	**DRIP TRAY** KEEPS GREASE AWAY FROM FIRE
	HEAT & SMOKE CIRCULATE THROUGH BARREL
	HOT ROD IGNITES PELLETS
CONTROLLER REGULATES TEMPERATURE	**INDUCTION FAN** STOKES FIRE **AUGER** CARRIES PELLETS TO FIREPOT

How pellet smokers work.

PELLET GRILLS

Pellet fueled grills (or smokers as I call them) have taken the outdoor cooking community by storm over the last few years and there's no doubt that they're here to stay. The pellets are 100% real hardwood which not only provides the heat but also the smoke for that authentic wood flavor that many of us crave.

Before we get into the various brands, shapes, sizes, and types of pellet grills, and there's a lot of them, we'll talk about the basic mechanics of how they work.

The Hopper

Let's start with the hopper that holds the fuel, the 100%-wood pellets. The hopper is often located on the side of the unit or sometimes on the back. These come in all shapes and sizes from smaller ones that hold less than 20 pounds of pellets to the larger ones that hold 40 or even 60 pounds, enough to continually cook for several days.

The hopper is designed to not just hold the pellets but to help guide them down to the mechanism that moves them from their holding cell to the burn pot where they can be ignited and create heat and smoke.

From the outside, the hopper usually just looks like a box. But on the inside, it is large at the top and gets smaller toward the bottom. At the very bottom is a small opening where you can usually see the mechanism, called an auger, that simply looks like a giant threaded screw. As the pellets fall down into the "threads" the auger turns and moves them toward the inside of the unit.

The Auger, Burn Pot, and Fan

The auger slowly turns based on the set temperature and other algorithms. As it turns, pellets travel from the hopper and fall into the burn pot where a red hot igniter makes them smolder at first, then burst into flames in order to create the heat and smoke needed to cook whatever is sitting on the cooking grates. The burn pot is located inside the cooking chamber, at the very bottom. It's about four inches in diameter and four inches in depth with a metal or ceramic igniter. The burn pot has a series of holes in the side of it that allow air from a fan to blow into the burn pot

Hopper complete with 100%-wood pellets.

intermittently, and sometimes at variable speeds, to help control heat and smoke production. This air also helps move the heat up and around the cook chamber. This process creates the basics of a convection oven.

Heat Deflectors and Drip Pans

Just above the burn pot is a heat deflector. Since smoking meat in general is all about indirect heat, even if it is sometimes at grilling temperatures of 450°F and up, such a deflector is essential here. The deflector forces the heat to move up along the sides of the cooking chamber, rather than just straight up from the burn pot, thereby creating a more even heat while eliminating direct and radiant heat.

Just above the heat deflector and below the cooking grate is a secondary heat deflector which doubles as a drip pan. This pan is usually sloped downward to catch the grease and other drippings and guide it into a trough on the side of the unit and ultimately into an outside hanging can or bucket where it can be discarded easily.

I recommend emptying the can or bucket just as soon as you are finished cooking so as to not attract uninvited critters.

Cooking Grates

As you'd probably expect, there's a cooking grate that sits on a ledge just over the drip pan. Sometimes there's more than one grate which is often an-on feature that you can take advantage of when purchasing a pellet smoker. If these extra grates come standard the more the better. Most pellet smokers are advertised as having a certain amount of square inches (in.²) of cooking space which is calculated by multiplying the width and the length of each grate and adding those numbers together to give you the total number of in.².

The Controller

The brain of the operation is the controller and like the other components of pellet smokers, most are quite similar from brand to brand. Usually there's a screen or readout that tells you the set temperature as well as the actual temperature. The power switch allows you to turn the unit on and off. A rotating knob lets you set the desired temperature, put it into a special "smoke" setting, or run a shutdown sequence where it burns up the remaining pellets in the burn pot and then turns itself off. On a few units, the controller uses buttons instead of a rotating knob but nevertheless, it works in the same way. On several of the latest models, the controller has one or more inputs for temperature probes which you can use to monitor the temperature of the food you are cooking. I will get into some of the less common features when we look at individual pellet smokers.

Smoker Body

We've discussed all the necessary parts that make it work but the skeleton or structure of the unit. This is the body of the smoker which is comprised of wheels, legs, cooking chamber, lid/door, and chimney. Pellet smokers are all made of metal in varying types and thicknesses and some have varying amounts of stainless steel which is nice since stainless has the reputation for outlasting regular steel and doesn't readily rust. It is very important to weigh these aspects of the smoker body when you are getting ready to purchase a pellet smoker. Another important thing to consider are the wheels and how mobile it is. This means you will have to ask yourself how you are going to use the unit and what type of terrain you'll be moving it over. Most pellet smokers are made to be semi-mobile on concrete

or hard, smooth surfaces but you can often upgrade the wheels or do a "competition cart" if you think you'll need to roll it over grass, gravel, or other less than smooth surfaces.

ABOUT PELLETS

Let it be known that not all pellets are cooking pellets!

Pellets designed for pellet stoves (heating) are made from lumber by-products whereas cooking pellets are made from very specific hardwoods that are known to be flavorful and safe for use in cooking. Make sure you do not confuse the two types or try to use them interchangeably!

Pellets are made by pulverizing and then grinding the wood into very small wood particles. The pulp is then pressed or extruded through small holes using high pressure. This pressing causes the wood to get hot releasing the natural lignin in the wood. Lignin acts as a glue that holds the pellets together. The wood is pressed into long rods which are cut into ½ to ¾ inch pieces and bagged and loaded onto pallets.

Now you know more than you ever wanted to know about pellets.

So how are these pellets used in smoking meat?

Aside from pellet smokers, pellets can very successfully be used in the same way that you use woodchips. I've used pellets in all my electric and propane smokers, and even occasionally mix them in with woodchips and wood chunks if I am short on chips or chunks or just trying to use a particular flavor of wood.

Pellets are also an excellent source of smoke in smoke generators such the A-Maze-N smoker tube and the A-Maze-N smoker tray, discussed on page 93. Pellets are placed in either the smoking tray or tube and then lit. The pellets flame which then goes away leaving a "cherry" that smolders and produces smoke for hours on end that moves from one end of the tray or tube to the other.

Instead of having to mix different types of wood pellets together such as pecan and cherry to get a certain flavor profile, many pellet manufacturers produce "blends" of flavors that are known

Camp Chef Woodwind SG

Grilla Silverbac

Pit Boss Copperhead 7 Series

to work well together. One of my most recent favorites contains pecan, cherry and maple.

I am always looking for good deals on pellets. When I can find them for 50¢ to 60¢ per pound, I'm a pretty happy camper.

PELLET SMOKER BRANDS

We've talked about the basics but there are some really big differences between some of the various brands and types of pellet smokers so here's a good spot to go over a few of these.

Pit Boss Copperhead 7 Series

To my knowledge, at the time of this writing, this is the pellet grill with the largest hopper and cooking space. It's not stainless steel, doesn't hold an exact temperature, and doesn't have Wi-Fi or Bluetooth connectivity, but it's a horse of a pellet smoker. It works exactly like all the others except that it has a 60-pound hopper and it has 6 racks that are almost 300 in.² each. That's a whopping 1800 in.² of cooking space. I don't know of any other pellet smoker that is that large or has that kind of capacity. The cool thing is that most of that space is vertical. The smoker stands about five feet tall so the actual footprint is only about 900 in.² This smoker also has a full-size glass door.

REC TEC "Bull" (RT-700)

If you're looking for a smoker that is decked out in lots of stainless steel, has a ceramic igniter which will last a lot longer than a regular ignitor, can hold an exact "right-on-the-money" temperature for hours on end, and connects to Wi-Fi so you can control it from anywhere in the world–then this might be the perfect pellet smoker for you. The thing is a beast, and just in case you're not convinced, it even has stainless steel horns on the front that serve as handles for opening the lid.

Camp Chef Woodwind SG

When it comes to features, this one takes the cake. It has a pellet dump system so you can easily change out pellets. The unit also has an ash cup that hangs below the cook chamber on the outside of the smoker so you can easily clean the burn pot without taking the smoker apart or getting out the vacuum. The trap door is opened with the pull of a knob and any ashes in the burn pot drop into the cup where they can be easily discarded. Voila! Easy as pie. This smoker also has a direct grill feature. The drip pan just below the grate has angled slots that allow the grease to run down to the trough and out to the grease

REC TEC RT-700 "Bull"

Traeger Texas Elite 34

pan. But if you activate the grill knob on the right side of the cooking chamber, the heat deflector is moved out of the way so the flames that are blazing in the burn pot are allowed to shoot up higher than normal. This direct heat comes pouring through those slots in the drip pan and up to the grate where that big juicy steak is just dying for some searing action.

Of course, while this is awfully cool, it's sort of redundant since this pellet smoker also boasts a sear box that is mounted on the right side of the smoker body and runs on propane. It is small but fierce and can produce up to 900°F of meat-searing heat. That cast iron grate will sear a steak and just about anything else to absolute perfection.

Grilla Silverbac

This is a pellet smoker I just received–and it has something that I haven't seen on any other pellet smoker. The bottom area of the cooking chamber is double walled which serves to insulate the smoker from the elements. This not only conserve pellets and burns them more efficiently, it helps to conserves heat in colder climates. Most other

pellet smokers require some sort of welding blanket or smoker jacket to help hold in the heat during harsh winters, but this one claims that it's just not necessary.

Traeger Grills

Of course we have to mention one of the first pellet cookers ever built by Joe Traeger back in 1985. Almost every pellet smoker built resembles the original pellet grills made by the Traeger company which were then designed to look a lot like a horizontal offset smoker with the hopper simply placed where the firebox would have been. Traeger is a solid name where pellet grills are concerned. While they are not as feature rich as some of the newer stuff coming out, I've had a Traeger smoker for about three years and never had an issue with it. Traeger has a very strong following and is still one of the best-known names among pellet grill enthusiasts.

PELLET SMOKING TIPS

TIP #1: To get more smoke flavor, start everything on the "smoke" setting. One complaint that I hear most often is that the smoke flavor is not strong enough when using a pellet smoker. This is because the wood pellets burn so efficiently that the smoke comes out cleaner. This results in less smoke flavor.

I have found that to get optimum smoke flavor when using a pellet smoker, you need to place the pellet smoker into it's special "smoke" setting for about thirty to sixty minutes right from the start and then after that, you can ramp it up to a normal smoke setting such as 225 or 250. Every type of pellet smoker has its own version of this special smoke setting which is designed to produce the most smoke in this setting and therefore the most smoke flavor. Using this setting will slightly increase the time on most recipes but you can easily offset that, if necessary, by cooking for the remainder of the time at a higher setting.

TIP #2: Use an A-Maze-N smoker tray (or tube) as described on page 93 if you need more smoke flavor. In a pellet smoker, the smoke is intermittent and more so as you cook at hotter temperatures. By offsetting this with the extra smoker, you can get a ton of smoke flavor into your food just as you can with any other smoker.

TIP #3: Don't get hung up on temperature swings. Most pellet smokers, except for the very few that have fancy controllers, are designed to swing by as much as 20 to 25 degrees above and below the set temperature. This does not hurt anything or cause the food to cook faster or slower. It's all about the average temperature. Your home oven works in the same way and if you don't believe it, just put a thermometer on it and watch the minimum and maximum temperatures for a little while. I have a very expensive Thermador oven that I use in my home (I didn't buy it, it came with the house), but it swings by about 25°F in both directions the entire time it's cooking. Still, it bakes wonderful bread, cakes, cookies and the like. What I'm really saying is that it's the average temperature that matters, so if it cooks half the time at 250 and half the time at 200, you are cooking equivalent to 225°F.

TIP #4: Aluminum foil is your friend. Use it to reduce cleanup. I recommend covering the drip pan of all pellet grills with aluminum foil–but just the inside so as to not impede airflow in any way. I purchase the 18-inch heavy-duty foil which is the perfect size. When you are done cooking, let the smoker cool down and then the foil can be removed, discarded, and replaced with a new piece, ready to cook next time.

STOVETOP SMOKERS

Before you say no to stovetop smoking, realize these smokers are not meant to replace your outdoor grill and/or smoker. Instead, they're a really great means to adding a little hint of smoke to things like fish, chicken, or vegetables, and perfect for folks who live in places that don't allow outdoor cooking, and/or for those who are not able to go outside because of health reasons. In these situations and more, stovetop units are lifesavers!

The set-up is extremely simple: You place a tablespoon or two of wood shavings on the bottom of the smoker. You then place the water/drip tray and then the cooking grate into the stovetop smoker. The covered smoker is set on the burner of your stove where the heat from the element causes the wood shavings to smolder and produce smoke.

I recommend lining the drip tray with foil to make cleanup a breeze.

I own the Camerons stovetop smoker and the

SPECIAL TIPS ON POULTRY

TIP #1: Always do a brine on poultry. This is what brine was made for and it does more for poultry, in my opinion, than any other meat. Don't feel confined to do a wet brine though since dry brining works equally well. And if you think that salt can't get through the thick chicken skin, think again.

TIP #2: Don't truss the chicken and you'll get better smoke flavor. When you truss a chicken, i.e. tie it all up so it'll look real "purdy," you are preventing the smoke from getting to all parts of the chicken. Just leave it un-trussed for better smoke exposure. "Truss" me on this!

TIP #3: For better chicken skin, air dry it in the fridge for several hours before seasoning. Here's the low-down: You are not going to get a crispy chicken skin out of the smoker. So instead, what you are looking for is good bite-through. To start off on the right foot, after brining the chicken, pat it really dry with a paper towel and then set it in the fridge, preferably on some kind of rack so air can get to it on all sides and dry the skin. You will notice that as the skin dries, it tightens and becomes thinner, paving the way for a better finish on the skin. This is demonstrated in detail on page 55.

TIP #4: For a faster and more evenly cooked chicken, "butterfly" that son of a gun. The correct term is "spatchcock." This just means to cut along both sides of the backbone to remove the spine, and then open it up like a book. This is usually done first thing before brining and prep. Cook spatchcocked chickens skin side up. Why spatchcock them? I literally thought you were never going to ask—this flattens out the chicken and removes the cavity making for a quicker and more even heating of the bird.

TIP #5: Mayo is the "wayo" to go to help your rub stick better. Before adding seasoning to the bird, apply a layer of mayonnaise to the outside of the skin. Mayo is basically a mixture of oil and egg yolks and the go-to binder for all poultry to help the rub stick and give it superb color and flavor.

TIP #6: Turkeys for smoking should be 12 pounds or less. Larger turkeys take too long to get out of the danger zone (see meat safety page 158). So if you need more than 12 pounds of turkey, smoke an extra turkey instead of a bigger one. Figure on about 1.5 lbs raw weight per person if you want leftovers. Example: a 12 lb turkey will feed 8.

HOW TO CRISP THE SKIN

Those of us who regularly smoke chicken know it is next to impossible to get crispy skin when cooking chicken low and slow in the smoker.

Sure we can crank it up to 350°F and get a pretty decent crisp on the skin, not like fried, but decent nonetheless. But then the chicken has very little smoke time and the smoked flavor you were looking for just won't be present.

So instead of crisp skin, aim for skin with a good bite-through. It doesn't have to be crisp, it just doesn't need to be leathery and chewy.

Dry the skin: To aim for perfect skin, it starts by drying the skin for several hours in the fridge right after brining it.

Whether you choose to dry brine or wet brine it, when it's all said and done, pat it as dry as you can with a paper towel.

Place the chicken on some sort of rack so the air can get to all sides. I recommend something like a cooling rack laid on a cookie sheet to catch any drips. Do not cover the chicken. Place the chicken in the fridge while it dries and leave it there for at least 3-4 hours–but overnight is so much better and will produce a better product.

After just a couple hours you will begin to see the skin tightening up around the meat as it dries and more so as it continues in the fridge. This is exactly what you want!

COOK A LITTLE HOTTER: The second thing you can do is cook a little hotter, maybe 300°F or so. This is only about 50 to 75 degrees hotter than normal low and slow, but it makes a world of difference. If you want to crank it on up even higher, you can certainly do that as long as you are aware that this also decreases the amount of time in the smoke–and I assume you are aiming for relatively smoky chicken flavor.

LEAVE THE WATER PAN DRY: If you are using a smoker that utilizes a water pan, leave it dry when cooking chicken. This is another great reason to brine the chicken beforehand and get some extra moisture into the strands of meat (see brining on page 144).

By leaving the water pan dry, the air inside the smoker is less humid thereby promoting more drying of the skin which is what is required in order for it to end up with any semblance of good bite-through.

High temperature grill or broil at the end: Another way to ensure that the skin ends up with a really nice texture that makes it a pleasure to eat is to remove it from the smoker just a little early, and throw it on a screaming hot grill, or under the broiler, for a few minutes to bring it up to temperature and to finish the skin with some high heat.

If you used a sugary rub or sauce on the chicken you'll have to watch it carefully to make sure it doesn't burn—and you will probably need to turn it a few times to get all sides right. Remove it from the heat when it reaches at least 165°F as measured by an accurate digital meat thermometer.

PEKING STYLE CHICKEN: Part of what makes Peking duck so great is the crispiness of the skin. You can achieve this in several ways, including separating the skin from the meat so the fat on the underside can render and drain off; making incisions in the skin to let all the rendered fat get out; drying the skin for several hours before cooking; and last but certainly not least, dipping it in boiling water for about 10 seconds before adding the rub and putting it in the smoker. This last suggestion really caught my attention and made me wonder if it would work on smoked chicken. Dipping it in scalding hot water or even pouring boiling water over the top of it immediately tightens the skin and begins the fat-rendering process. Be sure to dry it off really well once you dunk it in hot water—and be careful of splashing and spillovers!

BAKING POWDER AND SALT: Some people mix a teaspoon of baking powder with a tablespoon of kosher salt (essentially one-part baking powder with three-parts coarse kosher salt) and season the outside of the chicken with this. This raises the pH of the skin which helps the protein break down more efficiently, resulting in better, more crispy skin.

Use this method in place of dry brining so you're effectively "killing two birds with one stone." It works best if the chicken can sit in the fridge for at least 12 hours after application. Once finished, season with very low or no-salt rub or just some black pepper and herbs, and cook as usual.

You do not have to use all these methods to end up with great chicken skin but you should try to incorporate as many as possible to give the bird the best chance at perfection.

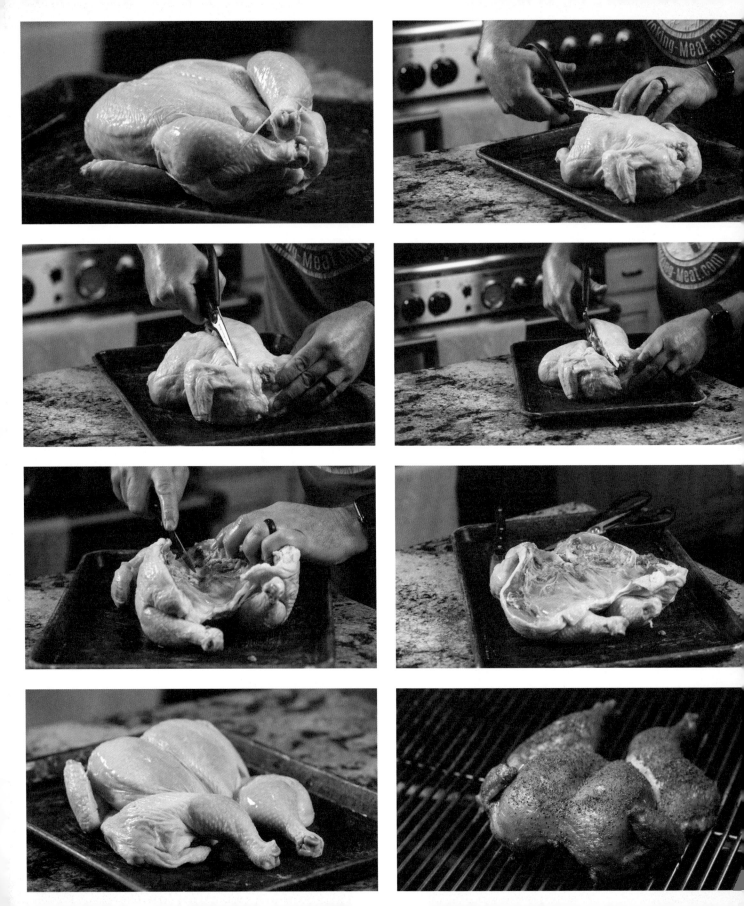

SPATCHCOCKING CHICKEN

Spatchcocking (butterflying) a bird is simply a method by which the backbone is removed allowing one to flatten the chicken out like a book. This method of preparing and cooking chicken allows the bird to cook more evenly and it gets done much faster. This method also results in breast meat that is not dried out, even if you choose not to brine it (see wet brining on page 144).

The word spatchcocking is fancy and I love throwing it out any time I get half a chance. And the best way to get to use the word is to cook game hens, chickens, and turkeys in this way.

To spatchcock any bird, you simply place it on a cutting board breast side down and, using a pair of sharp kitchen shears, cut along both sides of the backbone.

With the backbone removed, the carcass can be opened up like this book. Sometimes I make a cut into the keel bone but this is not absolutely necessary.

Turn the bird over so that the skin side is facing up. It can now be wet brined, salted as you would dry brining (see dry brining page 145), and/or prepared with oil, herbs, butter, etc. to get it ready for cooking.

TOP Nordic Ware stovetop smoker   **BOTTOM** Camerons stovetop smoker

Nordic Ware stovetop smoker. Both of these work quite well.

The Camerons model that I have is about 11 inches by 15 inches and is only about 3 inches deep which you might think limits what you can cook, but that is just not so. If you need to cook something that is taller than 2-3 inches, you can just use foil instead of the lid.

The Nordic Ware model is round and about 12 inches in diameter. It also has about 5 inches of headroom so you can do some taller items in it as well.

In this round stovetop smoker, use a regular 9-inch foil pie pan in the water/drip tray to keep it clean . . . It fits perfectly.

These stovetop smokers do not produce their own heat but rely on your stovetop, oven, or grill to produce the energy. I recommend medium-low heat to start and you can adjust from there once you see how that affects the temperature of the smoker.

I will tell you right up front that I prefer the Nordic Ware stovetop smoker hands down for several reasons:

- It is round and fits nicely on the burner of my stove
- It has a dial thermometer so I know the temperature inside the smoker
- It is more airtight and I can control the outflow of smoke if I want to via the vent in the lid
- The drip pan and food tray have a non-stick coating which makes it a cinch to clean

Let's do an experiment with pork ribs on both these smokers at the same time to give you an idea of how these work. I am going to cut a rack of ribs in half and put one half in the Nordic Ware stovetop smoker and the other in the Camerons so you can get a good visual of both units.

Go ahead and place both stovetop smokers on a large burner of your stove (over). I placed the Nordic Ware on the left front and the Camerons sort of straddling both the smaller front burner and the large rear burner due to its length; only the rear burner, however, will be turned on.

With all parts of the smokers removed from the smoker base, let's get them ready to smoke by adding two tablespoons of hickory woodchips. Spread the chips evenly in the center area of the smoker base.

With the woodchips in place, the drip pan can be inserted and filled with a liquid. I am using 16 ounces of water for this recipe but you can use other liquids such as fruit juice, beer, soda, whatever you like. You can also just leave the pan dry if you don't need the extra steam.

As you can see, I like to line the drip tray with foil or use a foil pan to help keep cleanup to a minimum. I am not sure if that makes me lazy or just plain smart!

The only thing left to add is the cooking grate and/or food tray.

Please note that I am using the cooking grate on top of the food tray in the Nordic Ware smoker. You don't have to do this but I feel this allows the smoke to get to the meat a little better.

With the smokers ready to go, let's prepare the ribs and get them on the smokers.

First lay the rack of ribs bone side up on your cutting board. Using a sharp knife or utensil, get ahold of that thick plastic-like membrane and pull it off. It can be quite slippery so I like to use a paper towel to give me a better grip. (Some folks use catfish skinning pliers for this task.)

Now, cut the rack of ribs in half, usually just between bones 6 and 7 and if it's not exactly half, that's ok too.

Nordic Ware stovetop smoker cooking set-up.

Camerons stovetop smoker cooking set-up.

Let's add some seasoning. I often use a rib rub that is sweet and spicy but you can also just use salt and pepper in equal proportions if you like.

Here's the rub I will use on this rack of ribs:
- 1 heaping TBS coarse black pepper
- 1 heaping TBS coarse kosher salt
- 1 level TBS smoked paprika (for color and flavor)

Pour about ⅓ of the rub on the bone side and spread it out real good with your hands.

Flip the rib halves over and add the rest of the seasoning to the meaty side, spreading it out with your hands like you did on the other side. Those pork bones are now ready to cook!

Place the seasoned ribs in the smoker and affix the lid.

On my electric range, I set the heat to "4" which is 1 notch from medium. You will have to experiment with your own stove to see what works best.

Within about 5 minutes I was seeing smoke and in another 15-20 minutes, the Nordic Ware was up to 200°F, my target temperature.

I assume the Camerons smoker arrived at that temperature or higher as well but it does not have a thermometer so you sort of have to fly blind with that one.

In about an hour, I lifted the lid just a bit and probed the ribs with my handy-dandy Thermapen Mk4 and they read 197°F and 201°F internal temperatures. A few degrees higher than I usually go so I made a note to check them at 50 minutes next time.

The color was pretty good, no crust really due to all of the steam but that was expected.

I laid them on the cutting board and sliced them up and although they were extremely tender, they cut fine and did not fall apart.

TOP Ribs cooked in the Nordic Ware stovetop smoker. **BOTTOM** Ribs cooked in the Camerons stovetop smoker.

The only other part of this experiment was to give them a taste so I ate one of the pork-cicles from each smoker and their flavors were very similar with just a hint of smoke, perfect seasoning in my opinion.

If I had to describe the flavor, I'd say it was much better than oven ribs but not nearly as good as what I can do in any of my outdoor smokers including electric, pellet, gas, charcoal, and wood. Having said that, if you are in a situation where this is the only smoke flavor you can get, it beats liquid smoke by a country mile and I'm betting you'll be pretty happy with the flavor.

SMOKING ON A GAS GRILL

Think you can't smoke meat because all you have is a grill? Think again! In this section, I am going to show you how to use your gas grill as a make-shift smoker.

Yes, it's easier to use a smoker designed for cooking low and slow but sometimes you have to use what you have until you can do better.

You gotta do what you gotta do and that's perfectly fine!

Smoking on a gas grill is just a matter of managing the burners so your food is getting indirect heat rather than direct heat.

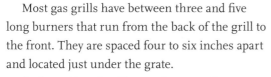

Smoking on a grill—Set-up A

Smoking on a grill—Set-up B

Most gas grills have between three and five long burners that run from the back of the grill to the front. They are spaced four to six inches apart and located just under the grate.

As I mentioned, with very few exceptions, smoking is done with indirect heat and to set this up, you simply light some of the burners to provide heat and leave one or more unlit. The meat or other food is laid over the burner that is not lit.

For smoke, you can wrap dry woodchips in a piece of foil with a few small holes poked in it to allow the smoke to exit. The foil pouch is placed in close proximity to one of the lit burners so it can begin to smolder and provide smoke. In some cases, it may be necessary to use multiple pouches to give you more smoke flavor.

Here are a couple of different configurations:

Another option for grill smoking is to use a pellet tray smoker such the A-Maze-N smoker to create smoke. This is a tray with a maze-like set-up on the inside. The tray is filled with pellets, lit on one or both ends depending on how much smoke you want, and set on the side of the grate to provide smoke while you cook.

The pellets will flame at first but then die down to a "cherry," much like the smoldering end of a cigar, which moves from one end of the tray all the way to the other over the course of 6-11 hours.

You will need a little airflow to the tray or it will die out. I usually set mine all the way to one side where there is a cutout for a rotisserie unit. You will have to locate the best location for your grill but once you do, you will find that it works really well.

Complete pictures and instructions for the A-Maze-N smoker are located on page 93.

SMALL EQUIPMENT AND TOOLS

When I first started cooking outdoors many years ago, I only had a cheapo dial thermometer, a used set of tongs and some worn-out leather gloves, but over time I have collected things that really help me with my cooking. I am proud to use these because they are high quality and do the job that they are meant to do very well. Most of these are not items that you absolutely need, but they are things you will want to purchase as you can to make cooking outdoors easier and more enjoyable. My wife calls many of these things "toys." I call them tools.

SLICER

A slicer is one of those things you don't really "need" but it's really nice to have. I made 17 pounds of bacon the other day and while I could have spent hours slicing all of that up with a sharp knife, a slicer made the job so much easier.

I don't have a high-dollar slicer. Although the full stainless steel models that can handle a huge piece of meat might be nice, mine cost just over a hundred dollars and does the job just fine considering I only use it once in a while.

I would say the more often you need it, the more you should spend so you get something that's really going to last.

Chef's Choice 609 slice

I have model 609 by Chef'sChoice and it does a perfect job for me. It also comes apart really easily so I can clean it—and for a slicer, that's one of the most important things in my opinion.

It came with a straight blade but I purchased a serrated blade since that sometimes works better for slicing bacon, my main use for the slicer.

If you're in the market for a much nicer one, like a Hobart for instance, and don't want to spend a lot of money, consider getting a used machine and purchasing parts to refurbish it. Almost all parts for the Hobart or similar quality slicers can be found through your friendly online search engine and it's much more economical than purchasing a brand new machine.

Another option is to check restaurants that are closing down, restaurant equipment liquidators, or auction houses that specialize in used food processing equipment–sometimes these places are letting things go for pennies on a dollar.

Excalibur 2900ECB dehydrator

DEHYDRATOR

I've used quite a few dehydrators in my time and I have a very good idea of what makes a good one and what makes a not so good one.

First and foremost, the ones that have a fan on the bottom and all of the racks stacked on top of it, not such a great idea. The very bottom layers get all the air and as you move toward the top, there's less and less air flow.

I recommend getting one that has a fan in the rear of the unit with shelves that slide in horizontally. In this way, the air blows across all shelves at an equal rate of flow making the unit work so much better.

I have been using the Excalibur 2900ECB for a great many years now. It has 9 trays, a powerful fan, heats up to 155°F and each tray is lined with a plastic mat that makes it really easy to clean up.

I line the bottom of the dehydrator with foil and change that out once in a while as well.

I like to do jerky as well as dried fruit and vegetables and, when my kids were smaller, I would

make fruit leather as well.

This machine also has settings for making yogurt and rising bread although I have never used these features myself. One would simply remove a few of the shelves in order to fit a container of yogurt or a ball of dough.

For making jerky, I often smoke the jerky for several hours first in the smoker and then move it to the dehydrator to finish. To me, this is the perfect set-up.

You can have a batch in the dehydrator while you're smoking a batch in the smoker and in this way, you can make a lot more than you could one batch at a time.

SPICE GRINDER

We call these "spice grinders" but I always use a "coffee grinder" for this purpose. In fact, many brands mention that their units easily perform both of these tasks. However, if you have a need to grind coffee, I recommend getting a separate one for grinding your spices so the flavors do not mix.

Whatever you want to call them, these grinders are quite inexpensive and can be found at big-box

Thermapen Mk4

ThermoPop

ThermoPro TP03A

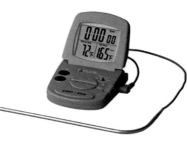
Taylor 1470

stores, online at Amazon, and any number of other stores.

I like to grind my own pepper, dried herbs, roots, etc. And there's nothing quite so fresh as when it's just been ground.

Both of mine are made by Mr. Coffee and cost around $14 each.

This is the machine that I use when I smoke/dehydrate habaneros and jalapeños and then grind them up into powder.

THERMOMETERS

I've met a lot of people over the years who say they don't need no stinkin' thermometer to tell them when the food is done. If this describes you then that's fine. You can skip this page. But for the rest of you, I highly recommend using a thermometer to really take your cooking to the next level.

A thermometer does for your smoker, cooker or grill what a speedometer does for your car. I've had a car or two in the past that had a faulty speedometer, one that did not work correctly or did not work at all–and that's just no fun!

I like knowing the temperature I'm cooking at, and I like knowing the internal temperature of the meat at all times. With all the technology we enjoy these days, accurately gauging temperature is really quite easy to do, and we have a myriad of choices surrounding us from the cheap to the expensive, all depending on what level of quality you opt for.

The more expensive ones will be made a little better, have some extra options, and will last longer but as I've said before, purchase the best you can inside your budget.

I recommend always going with digital over dial thermometers as these are more easily calibrated and just seem to work more accurately.

I have two different types of thermometers that I use, handhelds and what I call leave-in thermometers.

Handheld Thermometers

Handheld thermometers have a single job to do and that is to tell me the temperature of that steak, chicken, ribs, etc. and to do it quickly. I look for handheld thermometers that can read in about four seconds or less.

Thermapen

This is the daddy of all handheld digital meat thermometers, made by ThermoWorks, and it usually reads in around two seconds. This is great when I have 55 pieces of chicken on the grate and I need to check them all, fast.

This unit has an intelligent backlight that comes on when it's dark or when it's been awakened by movement. It has a 3000-hour battery life, has a splash-proof rating to IP67, an auto-rotating display, and it comes in 10 different colors.

Maverick ET-733

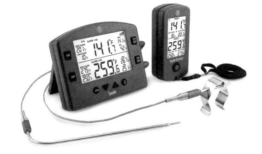

ThermoWorks Smoke

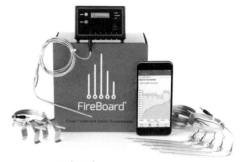

Fireboard

ThermoPop

A much less expensive model made by ThermoWorks, this one reads in just under four seconds. It has a backlight, rotating display, 5000-hour battery life, IP66 rating, and comes in 9 different colors.

ThermoPro TP03A

If you really want to go inexpensive you can get this handheld digital thermometer on Amazon for around $11. The accuracy is dead-on and it reads in about six seconds in my tests. It's not splash proof and doesn't have a backlight or rotating display but it does its primary job very well, just slightly slower than the ThermoWorks models. If care is taken, one of these could last for several years thereby making it a very economical solution.

Leave-in Thermometers

In the leave-in category, thermometers are broken down into wireless and non-wireless (when we say non-wireless, this means it *does not* connect to a base unit, via Bluetooth, Wi-Fi or other wireless connectivity, which you keep in your pocket). As usual, what you get just sort of depends on how much money you want to spend and how long you want it to last. There are tons of options out there but I'll just show you what I use most often and leave any further research to you if need be.

Taylor 1470

This is one of the first leave-in digital probe meat thermometers I ever owned and at one point in time, I owned six. These are non-wireless, run about $20 and can take quite a bit of abuse before they decide to quit on you. Nothing fancy, just a single probe attached to a four foot silicone cord which then plugs into the main unit. It has large LCD numbers and can function simultaneously as both a thermometer and a timer. Sometimes simple is better and these units are truly simple, do the job well and at a very reasonable cost to boot.

Maverick ET-733

This model has dual probes, a large screen, and is a little on the complicated side if you ask me. I never use the max temp or timer on this because I don't like having to read the manual every time I want to use it. Having said that, it is accurate, has a range of more than 300 feet, and comes with a base unit that stays right next to the smoker and another unit which you can place into your pocket or on the bedside table so you always know what's going on inside the smoker, temperature wise. The probes are connected to three foot-braided metal wires which plug into the base unit.

Smoke by ThermoWorks

This is the one that I use most often and it has a lot of features including splash-proof to IP65, dual probe, 300-foot range, 1800-hour battery life, 20

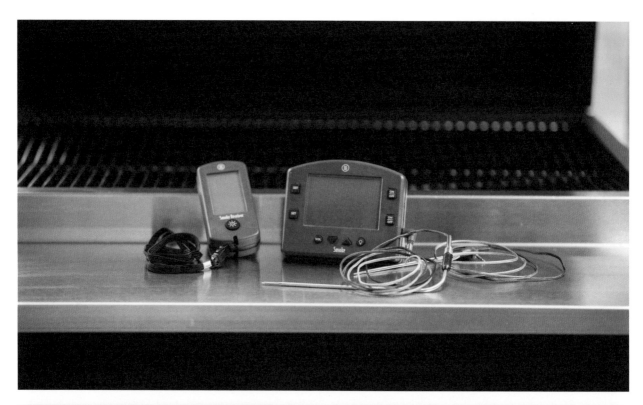

TOP ThermoWorks **BOTTOM** FireBoard

ThermoWorks Thermapen Mk4 handheld thermometer

second backlight, the ability to handle multiple remotes, and it comes in a variety of colors. This unit is extremely easy to operate and now has an available Wi-Fi gateway which can connect it to your home internet and give you accessibility from anywhere in the world. This means I can be at the grocery store and still read the temperature of my food and my pit right there on my smartphone for the ultimate in peace of mind.

FireBoard

This is a really sweet piece of equipment when you need to monitor multiple probes (up to six) at one time and be able to see them on your smartphone, from anywhere in the world via your home Wi-Fi network. The unit is rechargeable and lasts about 24 hours on a single charge. Not only does it measure the temperature of up to six items at once, it also has a special port that accepts a drive fan cable so it can be attached to a pit blower for temperature control. The probes that come with FireBoard are completely water proof although the manufacturer warns to not submerge them for long periods of time.

TEMPERATURE CONTROLLERS

Many of us old schoolers are conflicted: We don't have a lot of trouble maintaining the temperature in our charcoal smokers . . . But sometimes it seems like a lot of work . . . And wouldn't it be nice if we could just control it magically now and then . . . Well . . . Now you can.

There are a number of temperature controllers on the market today and most have available adapters that allow you to attach a blower to your smoker. The blower connects to a controller via a cable and once you input the temperature that you want it to maintain, it sends signals to the blower to produce air at variable speeds to hold the temperature that you've set. Some of these controllers are even smart enough to know when you open the lid and to adjust for this so it doesn't kick in at full speed just because the temperature suddenly dropped. This is especially important for smokers like the Big Green Egg which recovers fast once you close the lid. If the fan kicked in at full speed while the lid was open, this would cause the temperature to overshoot once it was closed again.

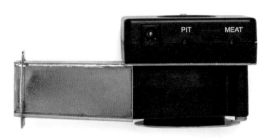

FlameBoss 400

PartyQ

CyberQ

I have several of these temperature controllers so let's talk about the differences.

FlameBoss

I use this temperature controller exclusively on my Big Green Egg XL and while the BGE is not difficult to control, it's really nice to know that it's being "watched" when I am busy with other things.

Like all temperature controllers, there's the controller, the blower, the adapter that attaches the blower to the air intake on the firebox or charcoal area, the ambient probe that attaches to the grate with a clip and tells the controller how well it's doing its job, and the food probe which tells the controller what's going on with the food. Using the signal from the food probe, the controller has the ability to bring the temperature down to keep it warm once it's done cooking. The FlameBoss connects to your home Wi-Fi so you can monitor and control the temperature of your pit from wherever you are.

On the newest FlameBoss unit, the controller and fan are together making it a one-piece design. It is controlled via a Wi-fi connection with a smartphone or tablet which is nice, but I do wish it still had onboard buttons for editing the temperature on the fly.

PartyQ

This temperature controller is manufactured and sold by BBQ Guru. It's unique in that it's a stand-alone unit. The blower and the controller are connected by a long adjustable "neck." It's battery operated and has a single probe that clips to your grate. I use this device exclusively on my Weber Smokey Mountain 22.5 by connecting it to one of my bottom vents. I simply set the temperature and it maintains that temperature for an indefinite amount of time or until there is no more charcoal left to burn. Because it's battery operated, I can take my Smokey Mountain on a camping trip and still have the luxury of controlling the temperature of my smoker with very little set-up.

CyberQ Wi-Fi

This is one of the models in the BBQ Guru line-up and it's the one I use to control my Meadow Creek TS120P. It comes with the controller, fan cable, fan splitter cable, two fans, two adapters, one pit probe, three food probes, mounting bracket, and a protective bag for the controller. It also connects to my home Wi-Fi so I can monitor and control the unit from anywhere. If you are in the wild, away from Wi-Fi or hotspots, the controller can also be connected directly to a smart phone, tablet, or computer for monitoring and controlling the cooking session.

TIMERS

Because most of us have a smartphone or watch that we use as a timer, we don't always think about having a device that operates as a dedicated timer. But these can be very handy to have, especially the ones below which feature multiple timers that can be displayed on a single screen.

These have magnetic backs and both are on my fridge at all times. Together, I can keep tabs on the cook time for seven different items.

Timestick Trio by ThermoWorks

This is one of two timers that I frequently use. It has a strong magnet on the back so it sticks to the fridge really well and it's also small enough to fit into my pocket. To make it even more useful, the lanyard allows it to hang around my neck if I'm so inclined. With three independent timers on a single screen, I can easily keep track of multiple items. Each timer has its own set button, and also a separate button for start/stop. There is also a full numeric keypad along with a lock button, light button, and a clear button so timers can be set and manipulated quickly with no need for time consuming arrow buttons. It also counts up and down, is water resistant to IP65, and comes in 9 different colors.

TimeStack by ThermoWorks

This "hoss" of a timer is supersized with large numbers you can see from across the room. It also sports four, yes four, independent timers each with their own set button and start/stop button. A full numeric keypad makes it easy to set timers quickly and there's also buttons on the front to control the backlight, the volume, time clearing, and recording a unique voice message that plays when the timer reaches its set point. For instance, if I'm cooking ribs, I simply hold in

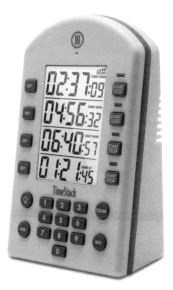

TOP TimeStick Trio BOTTOM TimeStack

the REC button and say, "The ribs are done you handsome devil" in my best Sean Connery voice and then, when the timer has elapsed, I have a simulation of the man himself notifying me that not only are my ribs done but that I'm one handsome devil. You just can't get better than that!

MITTS

Weber Barbecue Mitt

Wearing gloves or mitts or at least having some close by is a must when cooking outdoors. Messing with hot grates and live coals is dangerous and since we only have one pair of hands, it pays to protect them. Many barbecuers have their favorites though I recommend a mitt that goes up the arm a ways and is capable of handling extremely high temperatures. The Weber Barbecue Mitt is about the best thing you can use in my opinion. I keep one of these close by at all times when I am grilling or doing any cooking outdoors. It is 100% cotton and has a loop on the cuff so you can hang it up when not in use.

Pitmaker High Heat Meat Handling Gloves

These gloves are made especially for handling hot meat and hey, if you've ever tried to get a 205°F pork butt out of the smoker, that thing will melt your skin off! You need gloves like these to do the job right. With these gloves you can not only remove briskets, pork butts, ribs, and chickens from the smoker, you can also work with the hot meat right away. For instance, you could use these to immediately begin pulling the pork butts. Yes, I highly recommend these gloves. They are not really made for handling live coals and burning embers, but they will also definitely protect your hands in those situations regardless.

APRONS

Barbecue Apron

Aprons are often worn to protect your clothes from grease splatters and other food-debris mishaps. I'm not real choosy about my apron as long as it's black and as long as it has plenty of pockets for storing things I might need while

BOTTOM PItmaker gloves

cooking. Some of the best ones are thick, made of canvas, are washable and easily buckled in the back—not tied. I really like the ones made by Hudson Durable Products as they meet all of these criteria for a great apron.

KNIVES

Brisket Knife (top left)

It's important to have the right knife for the job and this is especially true for things like slicing brisket. You want a knife that's easy to grip and has a long sharp blade that will span the entire width of a large brisket. Mine is made by Mairico, is 11 inches long and made of stainless steel. It feels well balanced in the hand and delivers quick, precise cuts with minimal effort.

Filet or Boning Knife

This is a great knife for doing things like trimming meat and removing silver skin. And of course, fileting fish.

TONGS

Grillhogs Tongs (top right)

Ok, to say I am serious about my tongs would be an understatement—my tongs are my most used tool and if I was stuck on a desert island and could only take one barbecue tool, this would be it. These Grillhog babies are a massive 16 inches long which means when you are holding them normally, there's still about 12 inches from your hands to the tip. They also have oak trim on the outside of the handles for a cool touch. The tips touch when you squeeze them together and you can apply a lot of pressure if needed. There's a mechanism at the top that also allows you to lock them in the closed position which is great for storage in the drawer or hanging on the grill. I can slide these lengthwise under an entire rack of ribs and carry it in the house with no pan under it and no fear that the ribs will break off midway into the kitchen. Did I mention I love these tongs?

SPRAY BOTTLES

When it comes to barbecue and cooking outdoors, a spray bottle or two is a must. I usually keep one for misting the meat while it cooks. My misting bottle usually ends up containing plain apple juice, apple juice and apple cider vinegar mixed equally, soda pop, water, even coffee. As you can see, I'm not afraid to use almost anything to wet the top of the meat while it cooks. I don't spend a lot of money on spray bottles but I do make sure they are food grade which just means they are made of PET/PETE plastic or HDPE plastic. This is usually marked on the bottom and if it's not, I would just look for a different spray bottle. The one I'm using right now was obtained at the local dollar store and has lasted over a year.

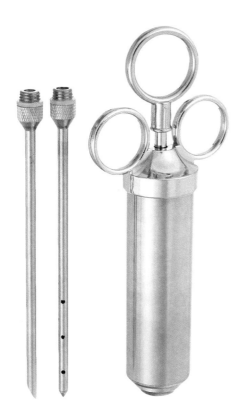

Bayou Classic injector

Ice chest by RTIC

INJECTORS

The One and Only Bayou Classic Injector

Most injectors are pretty standard with a container to hold the liquid, a plunger to push the liquid out of the container, and a tiny needle to transfer the liquid deep into the meat. I like to use things like coarse pepper and minced garlic in my injections so tiny needles just don't work very well as you can imagine. And that's why I only recommend this Bayou Classic injector with the huge needles.

It comes with two needles actually—one is open only at the very tip while the other is closed at the tip but has a series of small holes on both sides of the needle stem. I only use the one that is open at the end since it will allow me to deliver almost anything I like into the meat. Heck, I could inject some mashed potatoes into the middle of a meatloaf if I wanted to (which gives

me a very good idea). But I digress. You need this injector if you do any injecting at all or if you are looking to inject a brisket, chicken or perhaps a pork loin. You can read more about injecting meat on page 147.

COOLERS AND CAMBROS

Coolers, ice chests, cambros, whatever you call them where you live, come in all shapes and sizes and if you're anything like me, you have about 16 of these out in the garage because every time you go on a family outing, you can't find one so you just buy another—story of my life. Incidentally, they are a great way to rest and tenderize cuts of meat like brisket, pork butt, and chicken. This is also a great way to keep things warm when food finishes cooking just a little early. I cover more about using a cambro to keep food warm on page 150.

SPECIAL TIPS ON PORK

TIP #1: There are two types of pork—lean and fatty. All lean pork (except for ground pork) is done and safe to eat at 145°F and anything beyond this is simply drying it out. This includes pork loin, chops, tenderloin, and pork sirloin. When the meat is done, it will have a slightly pink hue to it. This is completely natural and does not mean it is undercooked. All fatty pork such as ribs and pork butt need to be cooked well beyond the safe temperature of 145°F in order for the collagen and connective tissues to break down and for the meat to become tender and juicy.

THE 3-2-1 METHOD

This is a three-stage cooking method for pork ribs and the numbers represent the hours in each stage. The heat remains at 225-240°F for all three cooking stages.

STAGE ONE (3 HRS.): Place the prepared ribs bone side down directly on the smoker grate.

STAGE TWO (2 HRS.): Remove the ribs from the smoker grate and place them bone side down on a piece of heavy-duty foil. I recommend the kind that's 18 inches wide and you'll need the foil to be long enough to completely encase the entire slab. Once wrapped, place back on the smoker grate to super tenderize the ribs via braising.

STAGE THREE (1 HR.): Remove the ribs from the foil and place them back on the smoker grate, bone side down. The crust gets really soft during the braising and this will help to firm the outside back up. This is also a great time to brush on some barbecue sauce if you want.

Spare ribs are much meatier than baby backs and therefore, the first stage for spare ribs is generally about an hour longer. The second and third stage are typically the same for spares and baby backs.

Once you've tried this you can adjust the tenderness to your own taste by increasing or reducing the time in stage two. If you add time, then remove that much from the first stage. Likewise, if you remove some of the time, add that much to the first stage.

For instance, if you decide to cook some spare ribs for only 1.5 hours in the foil during the second stage to reduce the tenderness, you would cook them for 3.5 hours in the first stage. This would give you a 3.5–1.5–1 method.

The third stage is always variable in that it doesn't have to be exactly an hour. If the crust is firmed up in 30 minutes and you want to call them done, then that is fine. Or, if you feel like they need more cooking time, you can cook them longer than an hour.

ABOUT PORK

Shopping for Ribs: When I go to the supermarket or meat market to pick up some pork ribs, I usually already know whether I am getting baby backs, spare ribs or some variation of spare ribs such as St. Louis style. I like to find ones that have a lot of fat striations in the meat but not a ton of fat on top of the meat. I know I can always remove it when I get home but I try to get something as close to useable as possible and then I can work with that. Baby backs are best when they are not so meaty. Meaty baby backs mean that there's a lot of loin meat on the top and while you may certainly think that's a good thing, it's absolutely not. Loin meat is perfectly cooked and tender at about 145°F while the meat under it, the rib meat, has a lot of connective tissue and is not tender and delicious until about 195°F. You can see how that creates a dilemma. If you want loin meat, purchase a pork loin or tenderloin. If you want baby backs, find ones that have no loin meat attached.

PREPARATION: Always remove the membrane on the bone side of pork ribs for a better eating experience. The easiest way to do this is to slip a butter knife between the bone and this plastic-like membrane to loosen it. Then use a paper towel to grab it and rip it clean off. If it tears, it's not the end of the world. Just get hold of it again and finish tearing it off.

Add the seasoning the night before for best results. I generally add a light coat of yellow mustard to help the seasoning stick and then apply a low-salt seasoning, lightly on the bone side, heavier on the meat side (opposite page).

SMOKING/COOKING: If you want less tender, not quite "fall off the bone" ribs, then just lay them bone side down on the smoker grate and cook them the entire time in that position. Use a thermometer to test the area between the bone, and when they reach 195°F, then they are tender but not falling apart and should have a great crust. To get them to that "fall off the bone" state that many people like, you can do what is called the 3-2-1 method for spare ribs or the 2-2-1 method for baby backs. This method is explained starting on page 80.

BBQ Guru rib ring

Weber rib rack

Dual beer can chicken rack

RACKS AND HOLDERS

This is a big category that falls under those things that you don't really have to have but are nice to have anyway. I'm talking about rib racks, pepper holders, cooling racks, grill pans, that sort of thing. I'm going to show you what I use and then you can decide . . . and go from there.

Rib Racks

I have no doubt tried every single rib rack known to man at some point in my career and I personally think all of them are made for baby backs or St. Louis style spares. They're just never tall enough or wide enough in my opinion. I don't use rib racks often but when I do, I usually am

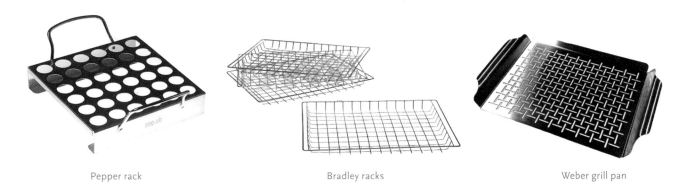

Pepper rack   Bradley racks   Weber grill pan

not satisfied with how the ribs sit. But sometimes when all you have at the campsite is a Weber Smoky Mountain 22-inch smoker and you need to cook five racks of ribs, rib rack it is. All in all, they are not ideal but it's the best way to cook a lot of ribs in a small amount of space. Most rib racks hold about five racks of ribs.

Beer-Can Chicken Thrones

Some like beer-can chicken and some don't but the fact remains that it does sort of look cool even if you really don't think it makes the chicken taste any better. I have been sitting chickens over the top of beer cans, root beer cans, and even soda cans for as long as I can remember just because it looks awesome and it's a great conversation starter. Quite simply, my guests always love it. The beer-can chicken throne is just a wire rack that holds the can and the chicken a little more steadily because, as we all know, making a reluctant chicken stand up just right is not as easy as we sometimes make it look.

Pepper Rack

I generally make stuffed pepper boats and lay them down flat but the special pepper racks you see at supply stores are made so you can cut off the stem cap, hollow them out, then stuff them, wrap them in bacon, and cook them upright. If you like to cook your peppers halved (boats) as I do where the pepper to bacon ratio is higher, then these racks ain't gonna bring you no satisfaction. If you cook them whole and upright, then this might be something to look into. The pepper rack that I inherited from somewhere holds 18 small to medium jalapeños.

Grill Pans/Racks

I have about 10 racks that come with the Bradley smokers and while I like their cookers, I like their racks better. I use them all the time, for everything. They are approximately 11 x 15 inches and fit in almost any of the smokers that I own. I like to lay them on the table where I am prepping the food and once the food is ready to cook, it goes into the racks. When I get ready to cook, I can carry the entire rack of food out to the smoker and simply set it on the smoker—no need to relocate everything to the smoker grate.

I also use the heavy duty stainless steel Weber grill pans as well as almost any cooling racks for this purpose. Once you get turned on to cooking this way, there's no going back.

BRUSHES AND MOPS

I'm not a huge fan of those little sauce spreaders that look like kitchen floor mops. In my opinion, the silicone ones work so much better, are easier

to wash, and I don't have to worry about leaving something behind when I'm brushing on the sauce. I have a couple of these from a discount store, a long one and a short one, and these do everything I need them to do and more where brushing and mopping are concerned.

CUTTING BOARDS

Cutting boards are usually made from hardwood, bamboo or even plastic and they sure do a great job of keeping the cabinet area clean and giving you a good, flat, solid surface to cut, trim, and prepare the food you cook. I recommend having several of these in various sizes due to the various sizes of food you prepare. If you're just slicing an onion, for instance, you can do with a small one, but if you are slicing a brisket or slicing up some ribs that you just pulled off the smoker, you'll need one that's quite large. I have collected several of these over the years and I'm not always as diligent as I should be about oiling them but I NEVER place them in the dishwasher like I've seen so many do. The best thing you can do for your wood cutting boards outside of keeping them oiled (food-safe oil only!) is to wash them by hand. In my experience, really large cutting boards are difficult to find. If you run across a good deal on a cutting board that looks like it could handle a 17-pound brisket and you can afford it, then go for it. Last word: One of the most useful cutting board features are those cutouts or gutters on the sides to prevent any juices from running off the board.

ACCESSORIES

Accessories are those things that work with your smoker or grill to help it cook just a little better. In other words, this list of items enhances the job your smoker or grill is already doing. In many cases these items are sold by the smoker manufacturer as add-ons while others are aftermarket products that have been invented and produced by other companies.

SMOKE GENERATORS

For our purposes here, a smoke generator is any device that creates smoke for the sole purpose of flavoring food. These can be either homemade or store-bought. Whatever the case, the purpose of smoke generators remains the same whether you choose to rely on your own ingenuity or just want a device that works.

Homemade Smoke Generators

Homemade smoke generators require a heat source and wood, of course. It is often important that the heat be minimal since these units are often used for cold-smoking things like cheese where you need smoke without any extra heat.

Most of the homemade units are made by placing wood into a coffee can with a piece of pipe

A simple mesh wire smoke generator you can make in minutes.

coming out the top, connected to a tee and then a short piece of pipe connected to both sides of the tee at the top.

If you remember the Venturi effect that Bernoulli discovered, well that's the idea.

Air from a fish tank pump is often connected into the short pipe on one end of the tee and as the air moves across the vertical pipe going into the can, it pulls smoke from the coffee can and the air/smoke mixture is emitted out the other side of the tee.

So where does the smoke come from?

Pellets or woodchips are placed in the coffee can on the bottom, holes are drilled to allow an inflow of air, and a larger hole is drilled to provide a spot to light the wood.

Once the wood is lit, it creates smoke which is then pulled up the pipe and out one side of the short pipes connected to the tee.

To use this for smoking meat, a rubber hose or something similar is connected to the end where the smoke comes from and that is then run into a box, smoker, grill, etc.–wherever the smoke is required.

This is a pretty efficient system that can be made for less than $25 with many of the parts found in the garage at home or at a nearby hardware store.

A much more basic version uses a sieve or wire mesh strainer. Push the center of the strainer up so it creates a valley all the way around the outside. Pour wood shavings or pellets into the valley, all around the pushed-up area and set the strainer into a pan.

Use a torch or even a small candle to light one end and once it gets going, it will burn slowly all the way around, creating smoke for several hours.

The A-Maze-N smoke generator is both simple and very effective.

Purchased Smoke Generators

If you want to just purchase a smoke generator instead of making your own, then perhaps you're like me and creativity isn't always your strong point. Fortunately, there are several inexpensive options that work really well.

At the top of my list are A-Maze-N products. This company has a tray that looks like a maze and when you fill it with pellets and light it, it provides smoke for hours.

I just happen to have one of these so let me show you how this nifty thing works.

Place the tray on a flat surface.

Fill it with pellets depending on how long you need smoke. Each row provides about 2.5 hours of smoke so do some quick math and get to filling.

You will notice a large hole on each end of the tray: This is for lighting the pellets. You can light one or both depending on how much smoke you want. If you light both ends, you'll have twice as much smoke but it will only last half as long.

Light one end for now and if you find that you want more smoke flavor, you can light both ends next time. I recommend a butane torch found at the hardware store, on Amazon, or at places like Harbor Freight or Princess Auto.

Hold the flame to the pellets just long enough to get a good fire going at the start of the first row. Then let it burn until it goes out. This usually takes 30-60 seconds.

Once the flame goes out, you are left with what is called a "cherry" that causes the pellets to smolder and create smoke. The cherry moves slowly along the row of pellets creating smoke for hours on end.

So once the tray is lit and smoking real good, place it directly on the grate inside your smoker, grill, etc.

Please note that you will need to place the tray close to a vent or opening of some sort as it needs a small supply of air or else it will die out.

So you think they're pretty cool and you'd like to have one? They can be found on Amazon.com or you can go to smoking-meat.com/amnps for a direct link.

The tray is really awesome and works like a charm in almost any smoker. But in small smokers with limited grate space, you may not want to give up any room to this 5 x 8 inch device. Fortunately, you really don't have to.

A-Maze-N Products also make tubes which work using the same concept but instead, they are simply tube lengths you fill with pellets. Light one end and voila, you have smoke for several hours.

Such tubes take up much less space and may be a better option for those who are space challenged.

These tubes can also be found on Amazon. com or via a direct link at smoking-meat.com/ amnts.

Both of these smoke generators are inexpensive, made of stainless steel and it is my opinion that they will last you a very long time. I've had mine for several years and I even throw them in

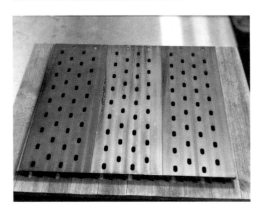

the dishwasher when they start looking cruddy just to shine them up again.

A small tip on the pellets: It is important that they are bone dry so I usually place the pellets into the tray or tube and set it in the smoker unlit for about 20 minutes while the smoker is preheating. This helps ensure that the pellets are dry and perfectly fit and ready for lighting.

Some folks place the pellets in a bowl and microwave them for 20-30 seconds to make sure they're dry. Both methods work well.

GRILLGRATES

These are comprised of long narrow pieces of anodized aluminum that resemble grill grates or rails on the top, but at bottom between the rails are "valleys" that are covered by a single row of holes or slots that allow heat through and up to the food. They come in a series of lengths from about 12 inches all the way up to nearly 20 inches and all are 5¼ inches wide.

GrillGrates are designed in such a way that they even-out and amplify the heat coming from your grill.

This not only gives you a much more evenly cooked piece of meat but you can get perfect grill marks. And because the mostly semi-solid bottom prevents flare-ups, the meat gets done perfectly without getting burnt. One of my favorite features is the ability to flip them over to flat-side up. This gives you a griddle-like surface right there on your grill.

I must warn you that these are not cheap, but I have a feeling they will last a very long time with proper care. Before ordering, simply measure the length and width or diameter of your smoker or grill. The measurement from front to back tells you the size of GrillGrate to order. Then divide the width (side to side measurement) by 5¼ to

Lone Star Grillz Horizontal Offset Wood Smoker (20 x 36 model) from lonestargrillz.com.

figure out how many will fit. Some customization is available at grillgrates.com if you need that option.

THE SMOKENATOR

If you use a Weber-style charcoal grill or kettle grill and ever wished you could find an easy way to smoke using indirect heat, then this device is for you. The Smokenator fits snuggly into the 18-, 22- or 26-inch charcoal grills and keeps your charcoal—as well as a small water pan—contained in a very small area on the side of the grill. You can then place your meat on the grate as far away from the heat as possible and close the lid. The lid should be situated so that the vent is on the opposite side of the Smokenator causing the heat

to be drawn up and across the meat. The instructions say to load the Smokenator with about 60 charcoal briquettes then remove 16 of them and light those in a charcoal starter (see page 120). Once these 16 pieces are partially lit, place them back into the Smokenator with about six ounces of smoking wood. By opening the lower vent of the grill all the way, or nearly all the way, and only opening the top lid vent on the grill about ⅜-inch (the width of a pencil), the grate will maintain a temp around 220°F which is perfect for low and slow barbecue. I always recommend purchasing an actual smoker if you can, but for those of you who already have one of these types of charcoal grills, this method is definitely something you can do for around $100 or less.

SUPPLIES

As you begin cooking outdoors on your smoker or even your grill, you will need things like foil, cleaning supplies, things to help you through the process. These are supplies that I recommend you keep on hand so you can cook something at a moment's notice without having to run to the store first.

Meat Wrapping Paper **98**

Aluminum Foil **98**

Foil Pans **99**

Cleaning Products **99**

MEAT WRAPPING PAPER

Rolls of paper are extremely useful for meat preparation—and even wrapping the meat while it cooks instead of using foil. But it's important that you purchase the kind that does not have a lining or a waxy surface. Unlike foil, paper is porous and "breathes." This allows some movement of air and smoke between the inside and the outside while still holding in some of that steam so you can get some braising action on the meat as well. In this way, wrapping paper is a nice compromise between wrapping things like ribs and briskets in foil versus leaving the meat naked throughout the entire cook. Pitmaster Aaron Franklin has been a major player in introducing the use of paper via cooking briskets at his restaurant in Austin, Texas and this method has quickly become a hot topic on most websites, blogs, and forums that discuss cooking outdoors—and more specifically, cooking briskets low and slow. I recommend the pink-colored paper in a width of at least 24 inches. The good thing is it's not that expensive and a roll will last a very long time—unless you are cooking for a restaurant, or an army, in which case, it may not.

ALUMINUM FOIL

Don't buy the cheap stuff. I'm as tempted as the next guy to purchase the one-buck roll at the dollar mart, but it will leave you hurt, rejected, and ashamed in the end—trust me. If you have a local club store like Costco or Sam's close by or even a restaurant supply store, you can get much better deals if you purchase this stuff in bulk.

So in spite of it being dubbed "the Texas crutch," why do we outdoor cooks use so much foil? Well sure, it's good for wrapping some things when they reach a certain level of done, but some of my favorite uses for it are wrapping water pans and other parts inside the smoker so I don't have to clean so much. I love clean smokers and grills and I do the grunt work when necessary, but I would rather work a little smarter instead of harder when I get the opportunity and heavy-duty foil gives me that flexibility.

Some other great uses for foil:

- Ball up on old piece around your ambient temperature probe and lay it on the smoker grate to get an exact temperature at grate level.
- Ball up an old piece in your hand and use it to clean the grates.
- Use small pieces of it to cover wings, legs, etc. to stop the browning process once those areas reach the right level of done.

Be sure to purchase the stuff that's at least eighteen inches wide and you'll thank me later.

FOIL PANS

I purchase two sizes of foil pans and I get them in bulk packages of 15 to 30 in a pack. I get half-size steam table pans and full-size steam table pans. I rarely have a need for other sizes. If I'm cooking a big ol' brisket and I want to place him down in an open pan instead of laying it on the grate, then that full-size pan will do the job with room left over. For things like pork butts and chickens, the half size is perfect. I often place these on the grate and set the food in them instead of on the grate. I have found that the smoke still finds its way down into the pan and it really minimizes my cleanup. Another option is to set a foil pan on the grate then set a cooking rack, such as a Bradley rack or any cooling rack, right on top of the pan. The meat can be placed on top of the rack and because it's sitting on a pan, the smoke easily gets to it while the pan catches the drippings. Of course, if you have a smoker with multiple racks, you can place the pan on a rack directly under the meat and get the same effect. Another great use of pans is when the food is all done cooking and you need to take it somewhere. These are a lot safer and more spill-proof than just wrapping it in foil. I

can't recommend enough that you keep these in stock–and once again, big club stores and restaurant supply outlets are your friend. I purchase mine at Costco for a fraction of what I'd pay if I was purchasing individual pans elsewhere.

I also use these foil pans in place of wrapping things in foil. For instance, instead of wrapping a pork butt in foil when it reaches about 160°F, I simply sit that butt down in a foil pan, if it's not there already, and then place another pan, upside down, on top of it. I usually don't bother sealing it but if you wanted to, you can use metal binder clips on the edges of the pans to lock them together.

CLEANING PRODUCTS

I'm not a fan of using stronger products than required, but as an outdoor cook, we encounter *a lot* of grease, and you just can't skimp on the stuff needed to clean that stuff up. Of course, there's no substitute for elbow grease, but that needs to be combined with stuff that works. Always use hot water when cleaning anything greasy and a soap that breaks down grease such as Dawn. I recommend Simple Green for the really tough jobs and purchase those plastic mesh scrubbers by the bag. They won't scratch but they do a great job loosening burned-on crud from your smoker grates and even your pots and pans. I keep antibacterial wipes for cleaning my non-waterproof thermometer probes since water kills those things dead if it gets between the wire and the probe. After cleaning, I rinse the probes with a damp paper towel and I'm good to go for the next time.

I use Watkins universal spray cleaner on the outside of my smokers as needed, just a good spray-and-wipe keeps them looking brand new.

ALL ABOUT WOOD

When it comes right down to it, next to the smoker, wood is one of the most important ingredients in your cooking since that's where the smoke flavor comes from. In this section we'll talk about wood, where to get it, what kind to use and even discuss methods of using it to get the very best smoke flavor.

WOOD AND FLAVOR

When it comes to smoking meat, our cooking devices are simply ovens that we use outdoors. What makes them different is the smoke that we introduce while we cook via real wood logs, wood pellets, woodchips or chunks, or just charcoal made from wood. I often get asked the question: What wood should I pair with a certain type of meat?

I don't necessarily buy into the theory that wood is like wine in that there is a certain wood that works best for a certain meat. I think most woods work with most meats and it's up to you to control the amount of airflow which in essence controls the amount of smoke flavor.

The more open you keep the vents, the faster the draft flows through the smoker and the less time the smoke just hangs around and flavors the meat. I can use mesquite with the vents open enough so that the smoke is not overpowering.

On the other hand, I can use alder and shut down the vents to very nearly closed so that the smoke is getting stagnant and the smoke flavor will be fairly strong.

I use a lot of pecan and cherry and I can tell you that most things turn out amazing with these two woods. I would still be pretty happy if these were the only types of wood I could get.

I have also noticed that the flavor profiles of a certain type of wood can vary from one source to the next. I have concluded (without any real science of my own to back it up) that there's a lot more variables affecting the flavor that wood smoke imparts to meat than meets the eye. For instance, how long the wood has cured, what type of soil it was grown in, perhaps the age of the tree, bark on or off, and so on.

Here's a list of woods that I've used over the years and the strength of the flavor they impart:

Type of Wood	Strength
Alder	Light
Apple*	Light
Apricot	Light
Black Cherry	Medium
Cherry*	Medium
Hickory*	Strong
Maple*	Medium
Mesquite*	Extra Strong
Mulberry	Light
Olive	Light
Orange	Medium
Pear	Light
Pecan*	Strong
Plum	Light
Post Oak	Medium
Red Oak	Medium

*Most common flavors

WOOD SPLITS

Wood splits or simply "splits" are created when you use a hydraulic splitter or an old-fashioned axe and wedge to separate a bucked-up log into 4, 6 or even 8 pieces, depending on the diameter of the log.

Most larger smokers such as the horizontal offset smokers, commercial rigs, and some of the larger cabinet-style wood smokers can use just wood, or a mix of charcoal and wood.

My Meadow Creek TS120P horizontal offset smoker uses splits of wood just fine, but I prefer to use lump charcoal as the main source of heat with a split or two of wood for smoke production. With this set-up I get better heat control as well as plenty of smoke for that truly authentic wood smoked flavor.

If you are purchasing wood splits or even cutting them yourself, make sure to know the dimensions of your firebox so they will fit properly.

In the Meadow Creek TS120P smoker that I use, the firebox is heavily insulated and is very efficient with fuel. I usually add a split or two every hour or so and only have to add charcoal a few times during a long cook.

The amount of wood used just depends on how hot you are cooking, the efficiency of your smoker, and whether you are using the wood by itself or in tandem with lump charcoal.

To make sure the splits are not wet when you place them in the firebox, and to get them hot and ready for combustion, set a few pieces on top of the firebox and the heat will dry them out real good while they are waiting to be used. Be careful though—if your firebox is not insulated, those wood splits can also get hot enough to catch on fire. In this case you may want to set a few pieces on top of the firebox for 8 to 10 minutes and then move them off again until ready for use. My wife has yelled at me more than once that "something was on fire on top of my smoker." So yes, I speak from experience.

ACQUIRING WOOD

I've been asked about acquiring wood so many times over the years, it just sort of burns in my

brain. People want to know where they can find good smoking wood without having to purchase it by the bag in the store. First and foremost, if you are going to acquire your own smoking wood, whether you just need small pieces or the bigger stuff, you really need to invest in a chainsaw to cut that stuff up. I figure it'll pay for itself over time if you are truly diligent about using found wood. The first time I decided I was going to cut up my own wood, I purchased an off-brand, inexpensive chainsaw. However, I spent most of my time working on that machine and very little time buzzing through wood. After a while I just went to my local Stihl dealer and got something that actually works. Starts first time, every time with minimal effort and all my chainsaw time is spent cutting up wood. I have no desire to be a chainsaw mechanic. I keep my chains sharpened and off we go.

Residential Cleanup

As you drive around town, out in the country, wherever you are, always be on the lookout for freshly downed trees or fresh tree limbs that have fallen into people's yards. Those who do not have a smoker see no value in those limbs that are falling from their trees and will usually give them to you if you clean them up. It would also be prudent to try and find out what kind of wood it is before you volunteer to clean up a bunch of limbs from a pine or some softwood that can't be used in the smoker. In the last house I lived in, we had over 30 pecan trees and if you know pecans, they drop a lot of limbs every time the wind blows. I gathered these up faithfully, cut them to size and even gave some away to friends.

Pecan or Fruit Orchard

If you happen to live close to an orchard that grows pecans, or some type of fruit such as apple, orange, or plum, then I am sure they prune their trees according to a schedule. It would not hurt to stop and ask them about helping "dispose" of some of that wood.

Furniture/Cabinet Builders

I say this very carefully because you have to be prudent when dealing with lumber to make sure there are no additives, paints, sealers, ink or other such materials on the wood that would make it unsuitable for use in cooking food. Having said that, there can be a vast supply of cherry, maple, oak, and a dozen other types of hardwood to be had at small cabinet shops or furniture builders—a possible goldmine for use in the smoker. Promise to bring the guys some ribs or brisket once in a while, and then make good on that promise, and you could run into a deal that could keep you supplied in good smoking wood for life.

Classifieds

Last but certainly not least, I'd be remiss to not sing the praises of your local classified ads along with Craigslist and Kijiji. Check the listings of these resources for free or cheap firewood and be willing to not only cut it and haul it away but to do a little cleanup as well before you leave with the free or nearly free wood.

GREEN VS SEASONED

I am a *big* advocate for only using wood in the smoker that has had a chance to season or cure. "Seasoned" is just a fancy way of saying "dried out." When wood is first cut it is full of sap, and if you burn it green, it creates lots of creosote and the flavor of the smoke is much stronger, more acrid, and just isn't as "smooth" in my opinion as the smoke from good dry wood. There are many

SPECIAL TIPS ON BEEF

TIP #1: Start with the best you can afford and you're that much closer to ending up with something really good. That may sound like a no-brainer. But I think some people still feel that since barbecue has its roots in using cuts that no one else wanted, then we should remain on that exact same path today.

Look, if all you can afford is scraps, then fine, because what you can do on the smoker with those scraps is incredible. But if you have the means and the availability to at least once in a while get a high quality cut of beef with a greater than average amount of fat marbling, then you'll immediately see the difference.

I have people emailing me wanting to know why, when they follow a certain famous pitmaster's brisket cooking techniques to a tee, they still turn out meat that is not as juicy as his, doesn't slice as good as his, etc. I just shake my head.

This renowned pitmaster is a great cook no doubt and could probably make a cowpie tender and delicious, but I happen to know that he purchases very special, all natural briskets for his restaurant—meat that's so much better than what I can find at my local grocer . . . even if it's prime grade.

Here's a mantra to live by where purchasing beef is concerned: If you're extra blessed, then go for the best.

TIP #2: Don't overcook beef if you don't have to. When I say "don't have to" I assume you know that some cuts are tender right out of the chute and others, like brisket, have to be cooked for a long time to reach that level of tenderness that leaves you saying, "You don't need no "teef" to eat this beef."

I'm not telling you how to eat your beef . . . if you like it well done then that's how it is. You eat it the way you like it. But I do wish I could talk you into at least trying a piece of good beef, cooked to medium rare and then at least you would have a proper comparison.

I know several people that grew up eating steaks and tri-tips cooked to well done and, after trying them medium rare, found that they actually loved them that way. Their barbecue lives were changed.

If you love it well done and covered with A-1 sauce then . . . I'll shudder quietly and let you enjoy it the way that you do.

So what about the beef that you have to overcook in order for it to be tender? Well, that's an entirely different story. We are talking about brisket, of course, and chuck roast, arm roast, the clod, to name a few.

TIP #3: Rest cooked beef at the beginning and at the end. What I mean by this is, let it come up to temperature before you cook it. A cold steak just doesn't cook very evenly and my ultimate goal every time I cook a steak is to have a good sear on the outside and perfect edge to edge color on the inside, whether that's rare, medium rare or, God rest that person's soul, medium, medium well, or well done, which is sort of a paradox for me since a well-done steak is not really done all that well . . . but I digress.

When the steak is finished cooking, it should be rested to allow the heat to dissipate a little and to allow the juices to redistribute throughout the meat. This makes for a more flavorful, tender, and juicy steak and is well worth the extra 5 to 10 minutes.

TIP #4: Always dry brine lean steaks for a couple of hours before cooking them. This is explained in detail on page 145. Once you try it, there's no going back. You'll be hooked for life!

TIP #5: Many people estimate how long it will take to cook brisket at 1¼ hours per pound. However, while this generally works out okay as an estimation tool, it's the thickness, not the weight, that plays the biggest role in determining how long to cook it.

HOW BEEF IS GRADED

There is a lot of science that goes into the grading of beef in regards to texture, firmness, fat marbling, color, and age. After taking all these factors into consideration, the beef is determined to be either prime, choice or select.

- Prime: Excellent fat marbling, texture, firmness and with an age range that is considered to be young and tender. Roasts and steaks from this grade are excellent for cooking with dry heat in a grill, smoker, or oven.
- Choice: Slightly less fat marbling than prime with good texture and firmness. Roasts and steaks from the loin and rib area will be excellent for cooking with dry heat in a grill, smoker or oven. Other, less tender cuts will also be suitable for cooking in a smoker, grill or oven but I recommend some braising and even

high humidity through the use of a water pan to help tenderize and keep the meat juicy while it cooks.

- Select: A grade I rarely purchase since it lacks much of the qualities required to make it flavorful and juicy. Most cuts are very lean and must be marinated, injected, and even braised during the cooking process to enhance the flavor and juiciness of the finished product.

In Canada, the grading is done in a somewhat similar fashion but with four high quality grades with Prime the highest category followed in order by AAA, AA and A.

A shield icon is placed on any packages of meat sold in the grocery store to show consumers the grade of beef so you can make better informed decisions on what to purchase for you and your family.

While you can usually find prime-graded beef in the grocery store, supermarket, and meat markets, the majority of beef sold in the local grocery store is graded as choice. Even though choice is of a slightly lower quality than prime, don't let that stop you from purchasing it and saving a few dollars where you can.

But all things considered, purchase the best beef you can afford and just go from there.

BRISKET PREPARATION METHOD

Cooking a brisket is a method, not a recipe. You can change up the seasoning or the marinade and you may even find a good recipe for an injection that takes the flavor up a few notches, but the trimming, cooking, caressing, wrapping, and resting of a big ol' brisket is a method that you need to get familiar with regardless of how these other things change from time to time.

Purchasing a brisket

There's a lot to be said for trying to find a brisket that's graded USDA Prime and hopefully raised naturally without hormones and such. You probably won't find the best brisket in the world at your local grocery store and this is where it's nice to have a butcher who knows where to find something "special." Of course, always give him a heads up about a week before you need it to give him plenty of time to find what you need.

As I just described, USDA Prime means that that animal was found to have a higher than average amount of fat marbling and other good characteristics. This is good because as that brisket cooks, those striations of fat will render between those muscle strands and will keep that thing juicy and flavorful.

TOP A beautiful three pound tri-tip finishing up on the smoker grate. **BOTTOM** Medium rare tri-tip. Notice the edge to edge pink that you only get by cooking it low and slow.

Does this mean you can't turn out a good brisket if it's graded let's say USDA Choice? Not necessarily, but you'll work your "rearward part that rhymes with mutt" off doing it and there's no guarantee that it won't end up a little dry regardless of what you do right.

I recommend buying a brisket labeled a "full packer" which usually means that it is the full point and flat with a fairly thick fat cap that covers the entire top side.

This means you can trim it, if necessary, exactly the way you want to when you get home—and that's a good thing

Trimming a brisket

I don't go crazy with trimming but I do some. You'll need a good sharp knife, something like a boning knife or even a fillet knife which has been known to work well.

You only need about ¼-inch-thick fat cap so I usually trim it down to that all across the top.

Also, there's a big pocket of fat on the side of the brisket, up close to the point which I usually trim down some but, then again, I don't get crazy with it.

Seasoning a brisket

I love to experiment so I've tried a lot of different seasonings, marinades, injections, etc. on brisket and really some of the best briskets are ones that are kept simple.

Most of the time, if I'm not using the Texas style rub that I sell, I just do a 50/50 mix of coarse kosher salt with coarse ground black pepper.

The Texas style is salt and pepper as well but with a few other things added in like garlic, onion, and a little cayenne.

So obviously, the meat side just gets seasoned real good, but what about the fat-cap side?

I think it needs seasoning too, but because it renders and the grease runs off while it cooks, I like to cut some grooves into the fat cap to give the seasoning a place to hang on. This also allows some of that rendered fat to seep down to where the meat is. That can't be a bad thing!

When you're doing the seasoning, don't forget about the sides.

With the brisket all seasoned up, you are ready to get started cooking.

I have a couple of brisket recipes in my last book, and on my website, so check them out and find what works best for you and your family.

varying opinions about this but since I wrote this book, just take my word for it and don't use green wood. Don't let your friends use green wood.

Green wood feels heavy for its size but if you keep it dry and make sure plenty of air can flow around it, after about 4-6 months it will begin to crack on the ends. If you pick up a piece, it will feel much lighter due to the moisture loss. At this point it is primed and ready for use as a smoking wood. Well that takes a while, but since you don't want to burn green wood, good things come to those who wait. Having said that, if you have a small smoker and you're mainly interested in chunks or pieces of wood, you can cut the wood up into the sizes you want and then dry it in the home oven assuming your partner or spouse doesn't mind the oven being used as a kiln.

Place clean pieces of wood on a cookie sheet in a single layer and place it into the oven preheated to 250°F for approximately 2 hours, or until you see the wood begin to crack just a little. I do not recommend exceeding 250°F and since you are using the oven for a non-conventional item like wood, do not leave the stove unattended.

You can also weigh a few of the pieces on a small scale before you begin and then weigh them again when you think they are finished. You are looking for about a 20% to 25% reduction in weight. When they are finished drying, remove them from the oven to cool. Don't eat them because they aren't cookies.

BARK OR NO BARK

The issue of leaving bark on wood is another subject that pitmasters will be arguing about for ages to come. It seems that everyone has an opinion about this, including myself. I have always maintained that if there is mold, fungus, rot, mildew, insect debris or anything else that makes me wonder if it's ok, or if the bark is already loose and falling off, I remove the bark. Otherwise, I don't worry about it. This is especially true if you are burning the wood hot. I'm a lot more picky if I know I'm going to lay that piece of wood off to the side and just let it smolder and crank out smoke for a while.

WOOD CHUNKS

Wood chunks often range from golfball size to fist size and everywhere in between. They also come in a variety of shapes. Such small chunks are a great size to have on hand and can be purchased by the bag at most hardware stores, sporting goods stores, big-box stores, and even your local grocery store.

If you have a band saw and a little time on your hands you can make your own by cutting splits into smaller chunks.

Two-to three-inch tree-branches can be cut to size using a band saw, table saw or a miter saw. If the wood is "green" or still has sap in it (freshly cut), it should be dried for three months or more out of the weather before using in your smoker.

I like to use wood chunks in combination with woodchips and/or pellets to get longer smoke times in my propane smoker.

I will layer the chunks on the bottom then pour woodchips or pellets on top to fill in the cracks. In this way I get an extra hour or two of smoke and don't have to open the door as often.

If you are using wood chunks in a charcoal smoker such as the Weber Smoky Mountain or even a barrel smoker like the Barrel House Cooker, you can place three to four fist-size pieces right on top of the charcoal for some really good smoke action.

If the chunks are golfball size, you can mix six to eight pieces in with your charcoal for

continuous smoke throughout the cooking process.

It is important to note that different types of wood produce different flavor strengths so when you are deciding on how many wood chunks to use, you will want to assume more for lighter flavored woods like apple and alder, and less for stronger flavors like pecan, hickory, and mesquite.

Like all things that get better with practice, keep good notes so you can adjust as you go and eventually you'll find the sweet spot.

Some people recommend a standard eight ounces of wood per smoke session and while this works great for some electric smokers such as the Smokin-it where you add the wood at the beginning and do not add more, I have not found this to be the magic number for all applications.

Woodchips

Woodchips, like wood chunks, can be purchased in most big-box stores, sporting goods stores, hardware stores, and your local grocery store. You can also order online if your local stores do not carry them or you are wanting more unique flavors of wood.

Woodchips are highly versatile in that you can add them by the handful right on top of the charcoal, or you can wrap them up in foil packs.

To make a foil pack of woodchips:

- Lay out an 18 x 18 piece of heavy-duty aluminum foil.
- Place a handful of dry woodchips in the center of the foil.
- Fold the top, bottom, and sides of the foil over the top of the woodchips so that you end up with a "packet."
- Use a fork or other sharp object to poke four to eight small holes in the top side of the foil so the smoke can escape.

If you are using a smoker or cooker like the Big Green Egg or other kamado cooker, you can mix in a handful or two of woodchips with the charcoal or you can pour a few woodchips in a spiral pattern right on top of the charcoal beginning in the center and working out from there.

Of course, like most other smokers, you can also place the woodchips in a metal box laid right on top of the charcoal to produce smoke.

Wet vs Dry

So the age old question remains—should the woodchips be wet or dry? Should the woodchips be soaked in water before use?

I'm honestly not sure where this practice got started but nothing is gained from soaking woodchips in water. Not only does the water not penetrate the wood, the water from the wood cools down the charcoal, takes longer to smoke, and finding a bowl to put chips and water into just gives you something extra to do when you already have your plate full just preparing and cooking the food.

To put it into perspective, when you place wet chips on top of the charcoal, this cools down the charcoal while the water from the wood turns to steam. As soon as the water is evaporated away, the woodchips then reach a temperature hot enough to create smoke. Seems very counterproductive to me unless you have a good solid reason to delay the smoke.

I have seen this practice on smoking and barbecuing websites, cookbooks, in smoker and grill manuals and even on TV cooking shows— and it's just a very unfounded process in my opinion. And I've even read that there may be some off flavors that can come from burning that wet wood.

Bottom line, use dry wood whether it's chips, chunks, or splits. Dry is the only way to go!

BONUS! THE UPSIDE-DOWN FIRE

This crazy one is controversial but I love it. And it works extremely well in certain applications even though it defies most of our inborn logic about fire building.

Having said that, I personally feel that the upside-down fire works best when building a campfire or starting a fire in the fireplace. While it can be done, it's probably not the best way to start a fire in your smoker.

I am sharing this with you because it's an awesome way to start a fire and I want you to try it— when it's appropriate of course.

You need some big wood that is about four to five inches in diameter, some medium sized pieces that are around three inches in diameter, plenty of smaller sticks that are an inch or so in diameter and, of course, you'll need a considerable amount of kindling, newspaper, dryer lint, whatever you regularly use and/or have on hand. I usually rely on newspaper but I'm pretty flexible and just use what I can find.

What I will refer to as a normal fire building process starts out as kindling on the bottom, slightly bigger stuff on top of that and then, once it gets going real good, some large splits or logs on top of that–and it's off to the races.

The upside-down methodology literally turns that fire-building process on its proverbial head by starting out with the biggest stuff on the very bottom. Three or four pieces butted up right next to each other will do. Next you have slightly smaller pieces, running perpendicular to the first layer and once again, butted up real close. Yet another layer on top of that of even smaller sticks, once again perpendicular to the layer immediately below it and butted up close. On top of those three layers, you have newspaper, kindling, small sticks, wood shavings, what have you. Spend a little time setting it up and it will reward you by burning for quite a while with little to no fire management required.

Light the kindling on top and once it's going real good just sit back and watch. As it burns, it will drop hot coals onto the layer below it and get that going and then as the bigger stuff gets going, larger pieces of red hot coals will drop down and ignite the wood beneath. I have seen fires like this last two or three hours. There are no rules that say it has to be three layers tall, you could make it four or five layers and no doubt get even more time out of it.

So how does this help you in the smoker firebox?

Well, you just condense it down a little but it works in the same way. Just make sure the size of the fire fits your firebox and smoker appropriately.

Start a wood smoker with a couple of medium-sized pieces on the bottom, on top of that place a couple of smaller pieces, then some kindling and small sticks on top of that.

Light the kindling making sure your vents are full open and once the fire is going, you can start closing down the vents some to get the heat where you want it.

I have used this method in my Meadow Creek TS120P with success. However, as I stated in the beginning, I prefer to save this type of fire building for the fireplace or a campfire.

For what it's worth, I prefer to use lump charcoal for the heat in my stick burners and place sticks of wood on top of the coals for smoke. See page 19 for more information on the Meadow Creek TS120P reverse flow smoker.

CHARCOAL

While there are many brands of charcoal, there are two main types—briquettes and lump, with each having their advantages as well as disadvantages. Let's talk about these two types of charcoal as well the various ways you can get the charcoal started for your smoker or grill.

TYPES OF CHARCOAL

When talking about charcoal, there are two main types of charcoal that are most common—briquettes and lump.

Everyone has their own idea about which one works best. I use both depending on what I'm doing, which smoker I am using, and so on.

Let's talk about these in a little more detail.

Briquettes

Charcoal briquettes have been on the market for more than 75 years as a way to turn waste wood products into cashflow. Briquettes were first pioneered by Henry Ford and his brother in law, E.G. Kingsford.

At that time, briquettes were simply made from wood scraps burned in an oxygen-controlled (more like oxygen starved) kiln and the charred wood was then ground and mixed with a glue made from potato starch and pressed into pillow-shaped chunks or briquettes.

At first it was sold to companies for curing tobacco and for fuel in ship kitchens and railroad dining cars, but later around the early 1940s, backyard barbecues became an icon of leisure and recreation and these pillow-shaped chunks of fuel found a new avenue of appeal.

Over the years the charcoal-making process has become faster and more efficient and other ingredients have often been added to the product including but not limited to coal, borax, lime, and even sodium nitrate, leaving us with a product that is not 100% wood.

And still today, thousands of tons of these briquettes are sold each summer as people fire up their grills, barbecues, and smokers to cook steaks, hamburgers, hotdogs, and even sliced veggies.

I personally don't like the ingredient list used in some charcoal briquettes, not to mention the petroleum products (lighter fluid) often used to get the charcoal started. Some say that the bad stuff burns off and maybe it does, but I'm not entirely convinced. I usually opt for the all-natural lump charcoal.

There are some briquettes that claim to be all natural with no fillers. When I opt for briquettes, I often use Stubbs as it claims to be 95% wood charcoal and 5% vegetable binder, which sounds like a much better list of ingredients. For set-ups like the Minion method (page 127) and the snake method (page 129) that tend to work better with consistently shaped briquettes, opt for more natural choices such as Stubbs instead.

Lump (opposite page)

Lump charcoal is made by burning pieces of wood in an oxygen-starved environment until all of the sap, moisture, gases and other impurities are burned up. What's left is lightweight pieces of charred wood that light easily, burn hotter than briquettes, and do not impart any off-tastes into what you are cooking.

The downside, if there is one, is that the lump charcoal consists of often odd-shaped, mismatched pieces of wood that do not burn as consistently as briquettes.

CHARCOAL LIGHTING METHODS

Regardless of what type or brand of charcoal you use, there are numerous methods that you can employ for lighting it up depending upon your situation, the type of smoker or grill you are using, and perhaps other factors such as convenience and personal preference.

Let's walk through your options one by one.

Firestarter Cubes (above)

The firestarter cubes that I use are white, come in a blister pack of 24 individually sealed cubes, and claim to be made of paraffin wax.

I have a theory that it's a different formula of paraffin than what you'd use for cooking . . . it just feels different and they do not melt in hot weather a you'd expect. Am I onto something?

There are similar varieties available that are mixed with wood fibers but you have to be careful as many of these warn not use them for lighting the barbecue.

The paraffin version lights quickly, burns for 8-10 minutes at a time, and isn't easily blown out by wind. I often use one of these under the charcoal chimney to get the coal going–and one is literally all it takes.

You can also bury two or three of these paraffin firestarter cubes down in the charcoal in your grill or smoker and light them to get the charcoal started. I usually place a few pieces of charcoal over the top of the cubes once they are lit making sure it can still get a little air. This is the method I use for lighting the lump charcoal in my Big Green Egg and it's ready to go in about 7-10 minutes. Not too shabby!

Charcoal Chimney (or "chimney starter")

A charcoal chimney or "chimney starter" as it's sometimes referred to, is the absolute best way to light charcoal in your smoker . . . in my humble opinion, of course. This is especially true if you like to use charcoal briquettes for fuel as these can contain ingredients that need to burn off before they get near food. By starting the charcoal briquettes in the chimney starter, you avoid the possibility of bad flavors and smells getting into the food or into the walls of your smoker.

I cover more about the ingredients and composition of charcoal briquettes in the Charcoal Briquettes section on page 119.

To use a charcoal chimney you will need:

- A charcoal chimney, of course
- A few sheets of dry newspaper
- A lighter or match
- Charcoal
- Leather or heat resistant gloves

Instructions for Turning the Raw Charcoal into Glowing, Heat Producing Charcoal:

STEP 1: Roll up a couple sheets of newspaper and then sort of twist and roll it into a donut shape. With the charcoal chimney upside down, place the "donut" of newspaper in the bottom of the charcoal chimney.

STEP 2: Set the charcoal chimney upright again and fill it with charcoal.

STEP 3: Make sure the charcoal chimney is sitting on dirt or on a paver stone or an area that can handle the heat without starting a fire. Light the newspaper via the holes or cutouts in the bottom of the chimney.

STEP 4: Be patient and wait while the fire lights the charcoal at the bottom and works its way toward the top. This can take 10-15 minutes.

STEP 5: When the charcoal at the top is glowing orange and fire and sparks are leaping from the top, it's ready to use. Put on your long leather gloves to protect yourself from the high heat.

STEP 6: Carefully pour the charcoal from the chimney into the firebox of your smoker.

Side Burner Method

If you happen to have a gas grill with a side burner, you can skip the newspaper in the bottom of the charcoal chimney and use the following instructions to get the charcoal started quick:

STEP 1: Fill the charcoal chimney with charcoal.

STEP 2: Light the side burner on your gas grill.

STEP 3: Set the filled charcoal chimney over the side burner.

STEP 4: When the charcoal at the top is glowing orange and fire and sparks are leaping from the top, it's ready to use. Put on your long leather gloves to protect yourself from the high heat.

STEP 5: Carefully pour the charcoal from the chimney starter into the firebox of your smoker.

Firestarter Cube Under Chimney Method

This method works exactly like the other methods except you light a firestarter cube under the chimney instead of using lit newspaper or a side burner from the grill.

The classic chimney starter which can be used for both lump and briquettes.

SPECIAL TIPS FOR "DOCTORING UP" STORE-BOUGHT BARBEQUE SAUCES

I recommend that every cook, whether you are a backyard chef or a classically trained professional, learn to create your own spice mixes, rubs, sauces, glazes, marinades, brines, the whole gamut. This is simply about trying new ingredient combinations, writing them down, and making adjustments until you get it perfect. One great way to start learning how to do this is by "doctoring up" store-bought products. I started out by doctoring up bottles of barbecue sauce I purchased at the local grocery store which gave me an opportunity to figure out what I liked and didn't like in a sauce and which later led me to developing my own highly successful barbecue sauce.

Here's some ingredients you might try adding to store-bought barbecue sauces to modify the flavor:

- Coarse pepper
- Minced garlic
- Red pepper flakes
- Your favorite hot sauce
- Coffee
- Cocoa
- Molasses
- Honey
- Soy sauce
- Worcestershire
- Sriracha
- Mustard
- Mayonnaise
- Cinnamon
- Cloves
- Your favorite soda pop
- Beer
- Wine

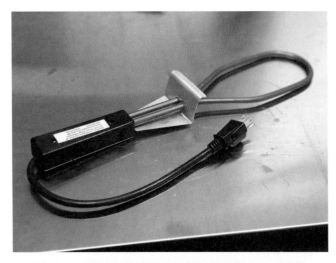

Electric Starter (left)

The concept for this is pretty simple. The lighting of the charcoal relies on a "U" shaped heating element attached to a handle that plugs into an electrical outlet. Power flows through the element at a certain amount of resistance and like the old incandescent light bulbs, more than 95% of that power is converted to heat. The element gets red hot and before you know it, you have a bed of red hot coals ready to cook up something good.

To use an electric starter, make a pile of charcoal in the charcoal pan or area of your grill or smoker. Then push the end of the electric fire starter down in the coals and plug it in.

Within just a short time, the coals will get hot and burst into flames and very soon, they will be glowing and ready to go.

Once the coals burst into flames, the fire starter can be removed and unplugged.

Heated Air

Believe it or not, you can light a fire with super heated air and yes, such a device exists that heats air to around 1300°F and as it blows onto the coals, it both starts the fire and fans the flames.

The original invention by Richard Looft of Sweden is sold in more than 27 countries. There are also several other companies making the product. The one I have is marketed by HomeRight.

This type of lighting device works especially well in my Big Green Egg kamado cooker where you only want to light a small amount of coals in the center of the fire. But it is designed for lighting natural lump charcoal as well as all types of charcoal briquettes.

My hot air lighter (as I call it) has a 10-foot cord like the original Looftlighter and a high temperature safety switch which will turn the unit off if it gets too hot. Once it cools it will begin working again.

To use, plug it in and hold the tip of the lighter against the coals while pulling the trigger. As soon as you see sparks, pull the device back away from the coals about 4 inches and continue to pull the trigger, aiming the nozzle at the same place where you began. In less than 60 seconds you will have a roaring flame. You can then unplug the device and set it aside carefully to cool before putting it back into its storage area.

TIP: If the high temperature (thermal) safety switch is activated, this is probably because it was not pulled back far enough away from the flames once the flames showed up. Let it cool off and try again, pulling it back farther this time so it can work properly.

Lighter Fluid

Charcoal lighter fluids have come a long ways and they're not all bad but there's still a lot of that petroleum based lighter fluid around so be aware.

First and foremost, there are much better ways to start a fire so you don't need it. Second, it's not healthy, doesn't really smell good, and you don't want that stuff getting on your smoker or grill much less the fumes getting into your food.

I know, I know . . . folks have been using this stuff for years and as far as you know, no one has died from it. Well, there's also no sense in taking chances with it when you have so many other wonderful options at your disposal.

If you are intent on using a liquid charcoal lighter fluid, use the ones that are alcohol based as they are better on the environment, evaporate quickly, and are just all around more "green."

TEMPERATURE CONTROL METHODS

The methods in this section are primarily for smokers that use charcoal as their source of heat. Charcoal smokers require a lot of tending and people with great minds, like Jim Minion, have developed ways to make it easier to control the temperature in this type of smoker by simply altering the way you set up the charcoal.

Minion Method Using Briquettes

First we have the Minion method which you may think sounds simple but prior to Jim Minion figuring this one out and sharing it, this way of lighting charcoal was unheard of.

As the story goes, Jim was cooking in a barbecue competition and sent his wife to a local shop to purchase a Weber Smoky Mountain (WSM) charcoal smoker.

On the morning of the competition, without reading the directions, he filled the charcoal basket with unlit charcoal then lit more charcoal and placed it on top of the unlit charcoal.

The smoker came up to temperature, he adjusted the vents and the thing held a solid 220°F for hours on end. He ended up taking a first place and second place in a couple of different categories and what we know as the Minion method was born.

The method has been tweaked since and I'm going to show you exactly how to use this yourself in a Weber Smoky Mountain or in any smoker, really, that uses charcoal.

In a WSM, fill the charcoal ring to the top with unlit charcoal briquettes.

PLEASE NOTE: You can also use lump charcoal and I will demonstrate that on page 128 but in staying true to the method, I will show you with regular ol' charcoal briquettes first, just like Jim Minion used.

Using a charcoal chimney, as shown on page 120, light up a few briquettes. How many you actually need to maintain a smoker temperature of about 240°F will depend on the weather and here's a reference that works for me:

Minion method using charcoal briquettes in the Weber Smoky Mountain.

- On normal warm or hot days, light about 20 briquettes.
- On cool, rainy days, light about 35 briquettes.
- On very cold days, light about 50 briquettes.

Pour the lit briquettes right on top of the unlit charcoal that's in the charcoal ring.

Place the body, racks, and lid back onto the bottom piece and set the vents. I recommend leaving the top vent full open at all times and the bottom vents 25% open initially.

Once the temperature climbs to 200°F, adjust the (3) bottom vents to maintain 225 to 240°F.

Remember that more air makes it hotter, less air keeps it cooler, but never close the vents all the way. It is really important that proper airflow gets to the charcoal and is able to exit out the top vent.

If you find that your smoker is getting too hot and your bottom vents are open less than 15-20%, then this means you added too much lit charcoal to the charcoal ring. The only option at this point is to remove some of the lit charcoal and place it in a fireproof container like a metal bucket. Don't extinguish the extra coals just yet as you might be able to add them back in later.

I recommend using large chunks of wood for smoke which are laid right on top of the charcoal

via the large side door *once* you are ready to start cooking. I usually wait until the food is placed on the grates before adding the wood.

Minion Method Using Lump Charcoal

The Minion method was designed for use with charcoal briquettes due to their size consistency, but many of us employ this method with great success using lump charcoal. Indeed, this book would be incomplete if I didn't show you how this is done.

I recommend filling the WSM charcoal ring with lump charcoal so that the fuel sits all around the sides but is low in the center.

Light about ½ a chimney of lump charcoal and once it's ready, pour it into the center of the charcoal ring . . . the lower area.

Place 3-4 large chunks of wood along the outer edge of the charcoal ring.

Put the smoker back together, replacing the lid.

Set the top vent to full open and the bottom vents to 25% open.

As in the regular Minion method, once the smoker climbs to 200°F, adjust the bottom vents as needed to maintain 225°F to 240°F.

Lump charcoal is inconsistent in size and quality and may not give you the really long burn

Minion method using lump charcoal in the Weber Smoky Mountain.

times that charcoal briquettes will, so keep this in mind. I can often get 4-6 hours using lump and that is still much better than having to add more lit charcoal every hour or two.

Snake Method

The snake method is another great way to control the heat over the course of several hours without having to constantly mess with it.

It's called the snake method because it, well, looks like a snake . . . sort of.

This charcoal layout is extremely helpful in the Weber kettle or similar cookers but it also works in other charcoal smokers such as the Weber Smoky Mountain (WSM).

To set up the snake, place a double row of unlit charcoal briquettes around the perimeter of the charcoal area leaving about a two inch open area between the start and the finish, then stack another double row on top of that one. If it's really cold, windy or rainy outside, you might have to add another single or double row. Then place wood chunks on the very top of the snake all the way around leaving a one– to two–inch gap between each piece.

Now, using a charcoal chimney as demonstrated on page 120, light 10-12 charcoal briquettes.

Once they are ready, pour the lit charcoal briquettes at the start of the snake making sure the lit coals are touching the unlit coals.

The initial lit charcoal will heat up the cooker and at the same time, work on starting the other charcoal that it touches. It will take several hours for the charcoal to light the ones next in line and so forth until it works its way all around the snake.

Remember the wood chunks we placed on top of the snake?

As the burning charcoal reaches each wood chunk, it will heat up the wood causing it to smoke, adding flavor to whatever you are cooking.

Methods like this are variable based on the weather, the type of cooker you are using, and even the type and brand of charcoal briquettes, so some experimentation is to be expected. But I can tell you from experience that this is the best way to set up a kettle for hands-off cooking over several hours.

SMOKING TECHNIQUES

Depending on your climate, weather, time of year, what type of smoker you are using, etc, you will use different methods to obtain the results you are looking for. In this section, I will also talk about seasoning a new smoker and how to know how much smoke to add to the food.

SMOKING MEAT IN COLD CLIMATES

Trying to operate a smoker when it's cold, windy, or rainy outside can present some challenges, but nothing that can't be overcome with a little thought and planning.

An important thing to note is that your smoker is going to take a lot more energy to maintain normal smoking temperatures when it's cold. This equates to more charcoal, more wood, more gas, more pellets . . . But there are things you can do to make the smoker more efficient in bad weather including, but certainly not limited to:

- Preheating the smoker to a hotter temperature than you regularly need.
- Placing bricks inside the firebox or smoke chamber (depending on the type of smoker that you have) in order to retain heat.
- Placing a welding blanket or other insulator over and around the smoker.
- Sheltering the smoker from wind and cold via plywood, cardboard, etc.
- Don't open the lid as often as you would in milder weather.

Many electric smokers are already insulated. However they will take longer to recover when you open the door to place the meat inside and/or if you decide to baste or mop the meat. I recommend you preheat this type of smoker to about 75°F hotter than you actually need. For instance, if you plan to maintain 225°F, then preheat to 300°F or as close to that as you can get. In this way, when you open the door to place the meat inside, even if the smoker loses a lot of heat, it will end up a lot warmer than if it had only been preheated to 225°F. Now place the meat inside quickly and close the door. Then drop the temperature to your set temperature of 225°F. I recommend you forego the basting if possible since this will add 15-30 minutes of cooking, based on the outside temperature, every time you open the door.

One way to save time placing meat in the smoker is first, find racks that fit in your smoker. Then place the food on the racks in your kitchen. When it's time to place the meat in the smoker, you only have to open the door long enough to place the racks on the smoker grates—which is much faster than fussing about arranging individual pieces of meat on the smoker grate. I use Bradley racks, Weber grill pans, and even regular cooling racks for this purpose.

To shield smokers from wind, you can cut a piece of plywood in half and lean the pieces against the smoker. Figure out which way the wind is blowing and make sure to block that side really well. In the absence of plywood, you can use large pieces of cardboard taped together with heavy-duty tape and then attach it to stakes in the ground to help keep it secure.

Another option is to purchase a welding blanket and place that over the top of horizontal-style smokers such as offset and pellet smokers. Sometimes you can find blankets specifically made for your smoker by the manufacturer or from Amazon.com.

SMOKING MEAT AT HIGH ALTITUDES

High altitude, which is basically anything above about 3000 feet, affects cooking, and if you live and/or cook at these elevations or higher, then you'll need to know not only how altitude affects your cooking, but what you can do to compensate for it.

There are three main things that are affected by high altitude:
- Atmospheric pressure
- Effective oxygen in the air
- Moisture content of the air

Let's take these one by one and discuss how they affect your cooking.

Elevation in Feet above Sea Level	Atmospheric Pressure in PSI	Boiling Temperature of Water in °F	Boiling Temperature of Water °C (rounded)
0	14.7	212	100
1000	14.18	210	99
2000	13.67	208	98
3000	13.17	206	97
4000	12.69	204	96
5000	12.22	202	94
6000	11.78	200.5	94
7000	11.34	198.5	93
8000	10.91	197	92

Atmospheric Pressure

Atmospheric pressure, also called barometric pressure, decreases as you increase in altitude. At sea level, it's 14.70 pounds per in². Just to give you an idea of the rate of change, above is a chart that shows how pressure decreases per 1000 feet of elevation and how that affects the boiling point of water.

As you can see, with decreased atmospheric pressure comes a change in the temperature at which water boils. While this affects wet cooking, like braising and boiling, more than dry cooking, such as smoking, grilling, and baking, it's still a factor that we need to keep in mind—and it can increase your cooking times, so beware.

Effective Oxygen

As we learned in grade school, fire needs three things to survive: Heat, fuel, and oxygen. At altitudes beyond about 3000 feet, oxygen begins to get a little more scarce and this of course takes its toll on fire. It takes more fuel to create the same amount of heat since each unit of fuel is putting out less energy due to decreased oxygen to burn. For this reason, it's important to allow a little more time for the food to finish cooking—and if it's cold or windy at altitude, you might have to wrap the smoker in a welding blanket or a special insulated jacket in order for it to cook at all. This will of course be more pronounced the higher you go.

Moisture Content (Humidity)

Air's ability to carry moisture also decreases with altitude so air is drier at say 5000 feet than it is at 1000 feet. So it's easy to see how this can also affect the outcome of food cooked in the smoker. Because the air is so dry, moisture will evaporate from the food much quicker than it would at sea level.

I recommend brining and/or injecting and plenty of rest time at the end to ensure that any moisture loss due to super dry air has been compensated for.

In researching this issue, many chefs say that altitude does not greatly affect the times of dry forms of cooking such as baking, smoking or grilling. However, I have heard many people who live at high altitudes say that it does affect them some. I think experimentation is the key to knowing for sure how altitude will affect

SPECIAL TIPS ON COLD SMOKING METHODS

There are many methods for creating smoke with no or limited heat. This is especially essential when you want to add some smoke flavor to things that melt such as cheese and butter. Cold smoking can also be incorporated into the cooking of steaks, seafood, and other lean meats such as wild game.

THE A-MAZE-N SMOKER TRAY

The method I generally use consists of a small, metal tray that looks like a maze. This maze is filled with hardwood pellets and lit at one or both ends. Once it catches, it can provide smoke for up to 11 hours or if you light both ends for more smoke, it will provide smoke for about five hours. This device also comes in a tube-shape version if you need to fit it into a smaller space. However, we will be using the maze version in our demonstration.

First, fill the rows of the maze with dry pellets up to the top or just slightly below the top, making sure there is no way for the fire to cross over into an adjacent row. If you are worried about the pellets being damp, they can be microwaved for about 30 seconds to remove any moisture.

If you only need a few hours of smoke, you can figure that each row will provide about two-and-one-half hours of smoke. For instance, if you need four hours of smoke, you can fill approximately two rows with pellets.

Set the maze of pellets on the lowest area of the smoker or box you are going to be smoking in and use a butane torch to light one end of the pellets. Hold the flame to the pellets until a good flame is going.

Let the flame burn until it goes out on its own. This usually takes about 30 seconds but a little longer is not uncommon.

Once the flame goes out, smoke will emit from the smoldering pellets. It's now ready to use. Carefully push the maze into position if necessary then the cheese, butter or whatever you are cold smoking can be put into place for smoking. You can find out more about this device by going to amazenproducts.com. (See also page 93.)

HOMEMADE DEVICE USING A WIRE STRAINER

This device is easy to make using an inexpensive wire mesh strainer that you probably already have or, if not, it can be purchased at a dollar store. Incidentally, this device works on a principle that is very similar to the A-Maze-N smoker tray.

I use a 6-inch mesh strainer but you can use a different size if you like. The center of the mesh strainer is pushed up so it creates a valley all the way around the outside edge. (See also page 90.)

Fill this valley with pellets leaving a one-inch gap.

Light the beginning of the circular row of pellets with a butane torch and once it's flaming, let it burn until it goes out on its own.

This device works best if it is propped up rather than sitting on its bottom where it's forced to support its own weight. Most of these have holders that stick out on one end and a handle on the other end. This can be set on cans, bricks, rocks, wood chunks, etc. to prop it up. Please note: If the handle is coated in plastic, the plastic must be removed so that only the metal remains.

A six-inch strainer will provide smoke for about four hours.

COLD SMOKING CHEESE

I think if people really understood how easy it is to smoke cheese, everyone would do it instead of paying premium prices for it at the grocery store. Now that we know how to rig up a cold smoking device, we'll have to locate some sort of box or enclosure to put the cheese in so the smoke can move over and around the cheese and flavor it. I normally use one of my smokers or a grill for this without firing it up or turning it on.

An old electric smoker that no longer works would be perfect for this as long as you have the racks for it. Place the cheeses on the racks with just a little bit of space between them. Get the smoke generator going and place it inside the smoker making sure it can get some air.

Keep the smoke going on the cheese for 4-6 hours and make sure the temperature inside the smoker does not get above 90°F. After the cheese is finished, vacuum pack it or place individual pieces in zip-top bags and store in the fridge for about eight days while the smoke flavors absorb into the cheese. If you taste it when it first gets finished smoking, it will have a strong smoke flavor and you might think it's too much–but letting it sit in the fridge will smooth it out and there will a big difference when you taste it the second time.

Smoked cheese makes great gifts or just smoke up a bunch and put it in the cheese drawer of your fridge for making sandwiches, smoked grilled cheese (amazing), smoked mac and cheese, smoked cheddar over scrambled eggs, and sausage (oh my), the list is long but you get the idea. Cheese is great on many things, smoked cheese takes it to a whole new level!

COLD SMOKING SPICES

To cold smoke spices I recommend pouring the spices such as salt, paprika, garlic powder, etc. into a shallow pan such as a cookie sheet. This will work best and be more potent if the spice forms a thin single layer. It is also important that the smoke be very cool and the heat be kept very low or at a minimum. Spices such as smoked salt may take as long as 8 to 10 hours to reach the proper color and flavor. I recommend stirring the spices every hour to make sure the smoke is able to access all sides of each grain or flake.

Once the spices are finished smoking, they can be placed into zip-top bags or lidded jars for storage. The flavor will become more balanced after a week or two. Items like this make great gifts but I suggest making them ahead of time so they have time to sit and mellow before use.

ONE THING TO NOTE ABOUT SMOKING SALT: Because it is essentially a rock, isn't delicate, and doesn't have oils like peppercorns and other herbs that can be released at high temperatures, it does not have to be cold smoked. Smoking it at 225°F is perfectly fine and still turns out an equally great product. This is great news for those who may not have a set-up for cold smoking or would just rather do it in the smoker, as is, at normal smoking temperatures.

your smoker and your cooking style. Check your smoker thermometers to make sure they are reading correctly then be sure to keep good notes on how long it takes to finish the things you like to cook. These notes will be invaluable the next time you decide to cook that same item.

USING A WATER PAN

Some smokers come direct from the factory with a water pan–and these things are not just to catch the drippings and keep your smoker nice and clean. Instead, the water pan serves several important purposes. In order of importance, they are:

- It acts as a barrier between the heat and the food creating an indirect style of cooking.
- The water gets hot and creates steam inside the smoker. This raises the humidity inside the smoker and slightly reduces the natural drying effect of heat. Contrary to what some have said, it *does not* add moisture to the inside of what you are cooking.
- The hot water in the pan acts as a storage device for heat and helps control the temperature inside the smoker. When the lid is opened and then closed, this stored heat helps return the smoker to its original temperature.
- Because water boils at or around 212°F (depending on your elevation), it is believed that this helps the smoker maintain a temperature that is perfect for low and slow cooking.
- And as noted, it catches drippings from the meat and helps keep the smoker clean.

I highly recommend placing heavy-duty foil in the bottom of the water pan before each cooking session and before filling with water to keep the bottom of the pan clean. This is especially important if the pan runs out of water as the drippings tend to scorch on the bottom of the pan and this stuff is very difficult to remove.

I tend to use water in the water pan if that is how my smoker is designed to function. However, many smoker owners have switched over to using sand, specifically play sand, since it stores heat much better than water and doesn't need to be replaced during the cooking session. This is especially nice for long cooks as it also helps regulate the heat over a longer period of time. If you decide to use sand, I highly recommend covering the bottom of your pan with heavy duty foil before adding it. Then cover the top with more heavy-duty foil to keep the sand clean.

When you are done cooking, simply remove and discard the top layer of foil and add a new piece in its place. The down sides to using sand instead of water is that you lose the benefits of having raised humidity in your smoker and the drippings will make a bigger mess since filling the pan with sand and covering it with foil essentially does away with the grease catching ability that the water pan provides.

I have not tried this but I have wondered if adding some water to the sand would give you the best of both worlds. If this is something you have tried I'd love to hear about it. Drop me a message on smoking-meat.com and tell me about it.

So what about smokers that do not come with a water pan but could use the benefit of a barrier between the heat and the food and/or more humidity inside the smoke chamber? You can add a water pan to almost any smoker or grill but you might have to get a little creative with it. For instance, I use the Smokin-It 2D which is a really nice, heavily insulated, Proportional-Integral-Derivative (PID) controlled, stainless steel electric smoker. It cooks really well but sometimes I feel that the food ends up a little drier than what I am used to from some of my other smokers. For this reason, I set a small foil pan of water right next to the woodbox and heating element to create some steam inside the smoker cabinet. I can really tell the difference when I do this.

In the Big Green Egg and other kamado cookers, you can usually place a shallow pan of water just below the grate. And even in pellet grills, I feel that some benefit is obtained from placing a pan of water in a location that allows it to get hot enough to create some steam.

It's completely up to you whether you decide to use a water pan, but I highly recommend you at least try it in your smokers and grills and see if it makes a difference in the outcome of your food.

HOW TO SEASON A NEW SMOKER

No . . . we are not going to add salt, pepper, and garlic powder to the smoker to "season" it!

Anytime you purchase or even build a new smoker, it is very likely that it contains oils, paints, and other chemicals used in its construction and I recommend that you burn these things off before attempting to cook with it.

As you've probably guessed, this burning-off period and getting the smoker ready for use is called seasoning the smoker. This is usually a one-time deal but of course I recommend repeating the process when you do a thorough cleaning of the smoker, one in which you clean the walls with a degreaser or cleaner to remove some of the built-up creosote.

The seasoning process also coats the walls of the smoker with that brown, slightly sticky creosote resin which helps prevent the metal from rusting.

So what does the seasoning process consist of? If you purchased a new cooker online or from a local store, it will no doubt have seasoning instructions that will probably tell you to set it up like you are going to cook with smoke wood at a temperature of 250-275F° for about 2 hours.

I have even seen instruction manuals for some smokers that say no seasoning is required—but I still like to go through the process just to make sure. After all, meat is expensive and you do not want any off-putting flavors ending up on your food. And the only way to make sure of this is to go through this seasoning process.

Please note that the seasoning of the smoker does not have to be performed as a separate process. The first time you are ready to cook on the new smoker, simply start about two hours early, bring the heat up to normal smoking temperatures of 225-240°F and hold that temperature with smoke for two hours.

You can also do a quick season at 350°F for about 45 minutes and obtain similar results.

Once the seasoning process is over, load it up with meat and let the fun begin.

To summarize, seasoning your new or thoroughly cleaned smoker serves one or more or the following duties:

- Removes any oils or chemicals from the surface of the metal
- Coats the inside walls of the smoker with creosote to prevent rusting
- Cures the paint

HOW LONG TO ADD SMOKE

Jeff, how long do I need to add smoke? I get this question several times each week—with good reason, people are concerned with how much smoke to add to their food maybe because they've read somewhere that you can over-smoke the food if you're not careful or that meat stops taking on smoke at 140°F and smoking it further is futile.

When I first got into smoking, ages ago it seems, I had many of these same questions and even adopted some ideas that were incorrect. I later learned on my own that there are a few myths floating around about smoking meat that are simply not founded on any fact. Let's deal with one of those:

Myth or Fact: Meat stops taking on smoke at an internal temperature of 140°F?

This idea would imply that at or around 140°F, the pores of the meat close up and smoke stops seeping in. The problem with this theory is that first and foremost, smoke does not seep into the meat via pores. It mostly just sticks to the outside of the meat and some of the sodium nitrate that is created when we burn charcoal, wood and/ or propane absorbs into the meat which is what causes that beautiful pink smoke ring. It stands to reason that smoke will keep on sticking to the meat for as long as it's in the smoker. Even in an electric or propane smoker, letting the smoke continue for as long as it's cooking best simulates what you would get in a wood smoker, such as a horizontal offset which burns wood, and/or a charcoal or pellet smoker which use 100% hardwood pellets both for fuel and smoke.

My smoke recommendation for charcoal, electric, and propane smokers?

In talking about smokers that use charcoal, electric or propane as fuel to heat the smoker, my general recommendation is to add smoke for at least half the estimated cook time. Whole chicken usually takes four hours at normal smoking temperatures so you would add smoke for about two hours minimum. A pork butt requires around 14 hours which would equate to a minimum of seven hours of smoke.

CONVERTING FROM °F TO °C

In barbecue and outdoor cooking, you will often find recipes online or even in books given in

°F	°C (rounded)
150	66
155	68
160	71
165	74
170	77
175	79
180	82
185	85
190	88
195	91
200	93
205	96
210	99
215	102
220	104
225	107
230	110
235	113
240	116
245	118
250	121
255	124
260	127
265	129
270	132
275	135
280	138
285	141
290	143
295	146
300	149

Fahrenheit (°F) only so it's important to know how to convert these to Celsius (°C) if that's the scale you are accustomed to using. I have included a handy chart (facing page) that covers the main range of temperatures that we use in low and slow cooking.

If you find yourself needing to convert a temperature that's not included in the chart, it's actually very easy. Simply subtract 32 from the F temperature then divide that new number by 1.8 and you're there.

Here's an example assuming I want to convert 375°F to Celsius:

375 - 32 = 343
343 ÷ 1.8 = 190°C
375°F converts to 190°C

PREPARATION METHODS

There are many methods for preparing meats regardless of how you plan to cook it, but for cooking outdoors, we generally use wet and dry brining as well as injecting as the top three preparation methods.

Pork belly brining in a cure so it can be made into bacon.

BRINING

Wet Brining

I have been brining the meat that I cook for about as long as I've been cooking. It's something I learned about early in life and I really enjoy the benefits it provides.

Let's talk about what brining is and then we'll discuss what it does for the meat you are getting ready to cook. And let me state before going any further that this is a great process regardless of whether you are cooking on your smoker or grill, or whether you are cooking in your home kitchen.

Brining comes from the root word "brine" which simply means water saturated or strongly impregnated with salt. Brining is simply soaking meat, usually poultry (but it can also be most any type of meat, even fish), in a salty water solution for several hours or sometimes even all night or for several days. Sugar and other ingredients can be added to the salty water to influence the flavor. To take things even further, liquids other than water can also be used. In this way, it can be as simple or as complex as you want to make it.

The salt content that I normally use for liquid brines is 6.25% salinity or 1 cup of kosher salt per gallon of water.

Sometimes when I mention kosher salt, people think this has something to do with Jewish dietary guidelines, but in reality, kosher salt was originally called "koshering salt" which has to do with its ability to draw blood out of meat. This same flaky, easy dissolving salt works great in brines–and that's why we use it. On more thing–I also like to put an equal amount of brown sugar in the brine to balance out the salt.

So what does soaking meat in a salty brine solution do for meat?

Explaining things of science has never been my forte but, in its most basic form, this process seeks to equalize the salt that is in the water with the salt content in the meat. Thus some of that brine salt makes its way deep into the meat fibers. Along with the salt, the meat also gets extra water as well as some of the other flavors, seasonings, whatever else you put in the brine solution.

When the salt gets into the meat it causes the protein strands to unwind and some of that salty water gets trapped between those strands. This is called *denaturing* and is an interesting topic to read about if you ever get bored watching your smoker.

Meat soaked in water alone will absorb that liquid but it will be lost during cooking since it doesn't get trapped in the fibers. Instead it gets out of the meat just as easily as it got in. When you involve salt, the water is trapped and therefore stays put during the cooking process. This means you end up with a much more flavorful and juicy piece of meat once the cooking process is complete.

Given enough time (and because of this equalization process I mentioned above), if the meat were left in the brine it would end up with a 6.25% salt content which is a lot more than what is needed. That's why we only brine for a certain amount of time depending on the type of meat, its size, and how much saltiness we want inside the meat.

I recommend you use my following brining chart for brining times. Over the years I've found that these times work perfectly for the different types and sizes of meat covered here.

POULTRY
WHOLE CHICKEN: 4 hours
CHICKEN PIECES: 2 hours
WHOLE TURKEY: 8-10 hours
TURKEY BREAST: 4-6 hours

PORK
BABY BACKS/SPARES: 6 hours
TENDERLOIN: 3-4 hours
LOIN: 6-8 hours
CHOPS: 3-4 hours

FISH
WHOLE FISH UP TO 3 LBS: 2-3 hours
FILLETS LESS THAN ¾-INCH THICK:
45-60 minutes
FILLETS MORE THAN ¾ INCH THICK:
90 to 120 minutes

SEAFOOD
SHRIMP: 30 minutes
SCALLOPS: 45-60 minutes

DRY BRINING

Dry brining is simply sprinkling salt on meat and letting science take over. Of course you need to know how much salt to use, what type of salt to use, and how long to leave it in the fridge.

Just like in wet brining, dry brining is a great way to get salt into the meat so it can help bring out the natural flavors.

I started out wet brining poultry, and then fish and a few other types of meat. But I started reading and experimenting with dry brining beef–and that process has slowly transitioned me over to dry brining almost every type of meat. In fact, I rarely wet brine anything anymore because

Salting meat for a dry brine.

dry brining is so much easier, less messy, and works so well.

To make it real simple, you sprinkle salt on the surface of the meat. The salt draws moisture out of the meat (a process known as osmosis) where it dissolves the salt and creates a slurry of meat juice and salt. This salty mixture is then drawn or absorbed back into the meat via a process called diffusion.

Another feature of using salt is that it is a good tenderizer. Proteins such as steaks, chicken, chops and the like are made up of bundles of long strands or strings very tightly packed together. Through a process called denaturing, the salt causes these bundles to relax, giving you a much more tender product. This relaxing also allows the salty solution that gets drawn back into the meat to go even deeper into it.

That is about as "sciency" as I'm going to get

and in a nutshell, it's all you really need to know about dry brining.

I recommend using Morton's coarse kosher salt for all brining since it comes in flakes instead of crystals and dissolves better than other types of salt.

You will want to use about ½ teaspoon of kosher salt per pound of meat but I've been doing it so much, I just sort of go by eye and it works every time. Of course, if you want to measure it out, there's nothing wrong with that.

Here's a thin steak above that has been sprinkled with salt. You can see the coverage that I used and this is what it should look like.

Thickness also matters. If I have a steak or chop that is more than about ¾ of an inch thick, I will first do one side and then flip it over and dry brine the other side as well.

Beef cuts like steak, ribs, even brisket, chuck

roast and tri-tip all benefit greatly from dry brining.

Likewise, pork cuts such as chops, ribs, loin, tenderloin, sirloin, and even the fattier pieces like pork butt and pork belly can benefit from dry brining.

But what about poultry? How do you get the salt up under the skin? Guess what? You don't have to. By some miracle of nature, when you dry brine chicken or turkey, whether it's in pieces or whole, you just salt the outside of the skin and place it in the fridge. Somehow the salt penetrates the skin and gets deep into the meat.

The first time you try this, I recommend using a single piece of something simple like a steak or even a pork chop. Sprinkle kosher salt on one side just like I did in the image and then place it in the fridge.

Wait about 30 minutes then go look at it. You will be able to see that the salt is melting or has already dissolved and the top of the meat will be very wet. This is that slurry I mentioned earlier. In another 30-45 minutes that liquid will absorb back into the meat and be ready to cook and eat.

I usually give it about two hours in the fridge. If the meat is over ¾ of an inch thick, I give it two hours on the first side then flip it over and give it another two hours on the other side.

Whole poultry such as chicken or even turkey can be salted and left overnight since it is important to also dry the skin before applying a seasoning anyway. This kills two birds with one stone . . . Pun absolutely intended!

Something worth mentioning is fat content of meat. You will most likely notice that any salt that falls on fatty areas (think ribeye steaks or spare ribs) will not draw any moisture to the surface and therefore won't dissolve. This is normal and no cause for alarm.

By the way . . . I have found that there is really no need to rinse the meat once you are finished dry brining. Most of the salt finds its way inside the meat and since the salt is properly proportioned, there is no need to rinse. You can go straight from dry brining to adding a low-salt seasoning.

I can't recommend enough that you try this. In my opinion, if it doesn't change your life, it will certainly change the way you cook meat.

INJECTING

What do you do when you're in a hurry and you don't have time to let the meat sit in a brine overnight or even for a few hours, but you still want to get some extra flavor and liquid into the meat? That's an easy one—you use an injector made specifically for this purpose.

In the tools section on page 79 you will see that I recommend the Bayou Classic injector which comes with dual needles that are both larger than what is standard in most injectors. The larger diameter of the needles lets you inject liquids into the meat that contain course pepper, small bits of herbs and spices, almost anything that you can think of that's smaller than the diameter of the needle.

To inject liquids into a piece of meat such as a brisket flat, pork butt or even a chicken quarter, I recommend wrapping the meat first in plastic food wrap. This prevents a lot of the mess since injecting liquid into the meat will often backfire and a geyser of whatever you are injecting will shoot back at you–and this is not pretty! I have learned over time that if I don't want to clean the ceiling, the walls and myself when I'm finished injecting, just wrap it in plastic.

Start with the injector plunger pushed all the way in. Submerge the needle in the liquid and

SPECIAL TIPS ON REHEATING

Because this low-and-slow method of cooking we call smoking meat takes so darn long, there is often a need to cook food ahead of time and then reheat it. There's also the issue of leftovers. But how do you reheat the food and make it taste like it just came off the smoker?

Well, most of the things that we cook low and slow also reheat really well– but some things do not. There're a few tricks I've learned over the years to make almost anything turn out wonderful–even if you have to "reheat to eat."

First and foremost, treat reheating with the low and slow still in mind.

FAUX VIDE

Sous vide in its most basic form is simply sealing food inside of a container, usually a vacuum sealed bag, and then placing it down in temperature-controlled water. This cooks the food to very precise temperatures over long periods of time. The result is perfectly cooked meats with no moisture loss.

Faux vide, a similar process, while not for cooking food, is a really cool way to reheat smoked meat—usually in an insulated cooler or cambro.

The meat, such as a brisket, is sealed inside a plastic bag (vacuum sealed usually), placed in the bottom of the cooler and boiling hot water is poured over the top to cover. The lid is closed and in about 2-3 hours, it will be heated through and through to a perfect eating temperature.

This can be done with almost any meat that needs to be reheated. It just needs to be sealed water-tight. It could get messy if it wasn't.

This works great if you want to cook a brisket, turkey, pulled pork, etc. ahead of time and you need to travel with it, perhaps to grandma's house. Place the cooler in the trunk of your car or bed of your truck, put the meat in the cooler, pour boiling water over it to cover, close the lid and off you go. Depending on how long of a drive it is, you could time it so that it's ready to eat at about the same time you arrive. Or keep the meat chilled in the cooler and begin the faux vide process at your destination.

OVEN REHEATING

I usually reheat at 275°F–no higher than that. This means it can take 30 to 60 minutes to bring food up to a good eating temperature. But it's worth it because the lower temperatures do a better job of reheating most proteins without drying the meat out like you would using a hot and fast reheating method.

For all intents and purposes, "a good eating temperature" can differ from person to person but I recommend about 130°F—still good and hot but low enough so as to not dry out the meat more than necessary–and it doesn't take things like steak beyond medium rare. I still use a thermometer for accuracy when I am reheating just like I do when I am doing the initial cook.

Also the time necessary to reheat is quite variable depending on how much meat is in the pan, how cold it is, how tightly packed it is, etc. Most half-size steam table pans full of meat can reach a decent eating temperature in 30-45 minutes at 275°F so let's just assume that you will be using the half-size steam pan and food portion for all the following recommendations for reheating in an oven.

The following are my tips for reheating specific smoked meats:

Pork/Beef Ribs

Ribs are one of the exceptions to the low and slow reheat rule. While they'll do just fine (sliced or whole) in a covered pan in the oven like most other things, they also do exceptionally well on the grill.

If you know you are going to reheat the ribs on the grill, forego the sauce during the initial cooking stage then, during the last few minutes of the reheat on the grill, you can brush the sauce on and let it caramelize a little. The ribs are done when they are heated through to a good eating temperature.

Brisket

I highly recommend faux vide for brisket if you have it vacuum sealed. Otherwise it should be sliced when it's done cooking and then when you are ready to reheat in the oven, pour some beef stock over the slices and cover the pan with foil. It's done when it reaches a good eating temperature.

Pulled Pork

I highly recommend pulling or shredding the meat just as soon as it cools enough from the initial cook. Freeze or keep in the fridge for a couple of days if you are going to need it soon.

If you know you are going to reheat, cut a stick of butter into eight pieces and place randomly across the top of the pulled pork. Then sprinkle about a cup of low-salt barbecue rub over the top of the pulled pork and cover with foil. When you reheat in the oven, the butter will melt and pull the rub down into the pulled pork with it. If you don't tell anyone, they'll never know it was cooked ahead of time.

Chicken, Turkey, Cornish Hens . . .

Place chicken in a foil pan with about ⅛-inch of chicken broth, water, or even something like apple juice in the bottom of the pan. Cover tightly with foil and place in oven. Once the chicken reaches a good eating temperature, open the foil and give it about 15 more minutes of open-air oven heat to make sure the skin is as good as it can be.

NOTE: Because of the elevated risk of illness when eating improperly cooked and stored poultry, I feel compelled to tell you that the USDA and most other food-safety agencies recommend cooking chicken to 165°F and then if reheating it, take it once again to 165°F. This may be necessary if you do not get it cool and then into the fridge as quickly as possible after the initial cooking. My suggestion is to be cognizant of the risks and get the poultry cooled and into the fridge as quickly as you possibly can. Then when you only heat it to a good eating temperature to preserve the moisture and freshness, it will be perfectly safe. If you have any doubts at all, heat it to 165°F.

Chicken Wings

These boys have their own category because I love them dearly and it's very important to me that you reheat them properly. They deserve that much respect. These do best if you reheat them hot and uncovered. Preheat the oven to 375°F and while it's preheating, bring the chicken wings out of the fridge and place them on a cookie sheet making sure they aren't too crowded. Just as soon as the oven is ready, get them in there. Flip them over after about seven minutes to make sure both sides get heated evenly.

KEEPING IT WARM IN A CAMBRO

All too often in cooking low and slow, we run into situations where we need to keep food warm for a little while, sometimes a few hours, and in case you're not

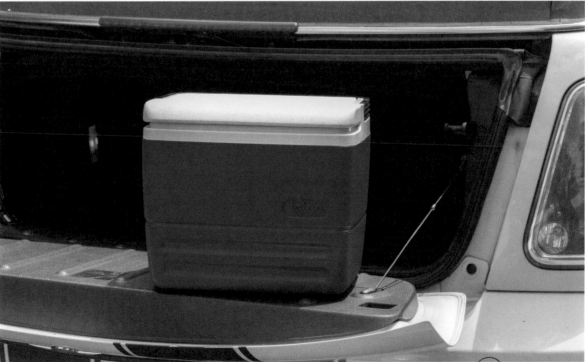

Keeping things warm for the road.

in the know, this is very easy to do with that cooler or cambro you probably already have out in the garage or attic–you might even have several of them.

I'm in that category of those who have a bunch—I haven't counted but it's probably safe to say I have eight or even 10 of these coolers. If you're reading this book and you live close to me or you're driving through, drop by and I'll give you one, Scout's honor!

These coolers are insulated and do a great job of maintaining the temperature inside the cooler. This is especially true for keeping things cold, but they also work really well for keeping things like briskets, pork butts, and ribs hot until it's time to serve. Heck, I often get the food done early on purpose just so I can place it in the cooler for a few hours. It just seems to get a little more tender while it's in there.

I recommend placing the meat in a foil steam table pan and covering it tightly with foil. Then sit the meat down in the cooler. The pan ensures that if it leaks, it's at least contained. This is important if you have more than one pan in the cooler.

I then fill in any remaining space with things that will insulate such as newspaper, towels, small pillows, etc. And close the lid. This set-up will keep something like a brisket or pork butt steaming hot for 4+ hours.

One thing to keep in mind is that the meat is not only staying warm, it is continuing to tenderize while in the cooler. So if I know I am going to be keeping the meat warm for more than an hour or so, I will remove the meat from the smoker a little sooner than normal since I know it's going to continue tenderizing in the cooler.

This method is also great for traveling with food. You can simply get the meat done early, place it in the cooler then load the cooler in your vehicle. When you arrive it will be steaming hot and ready to serve.

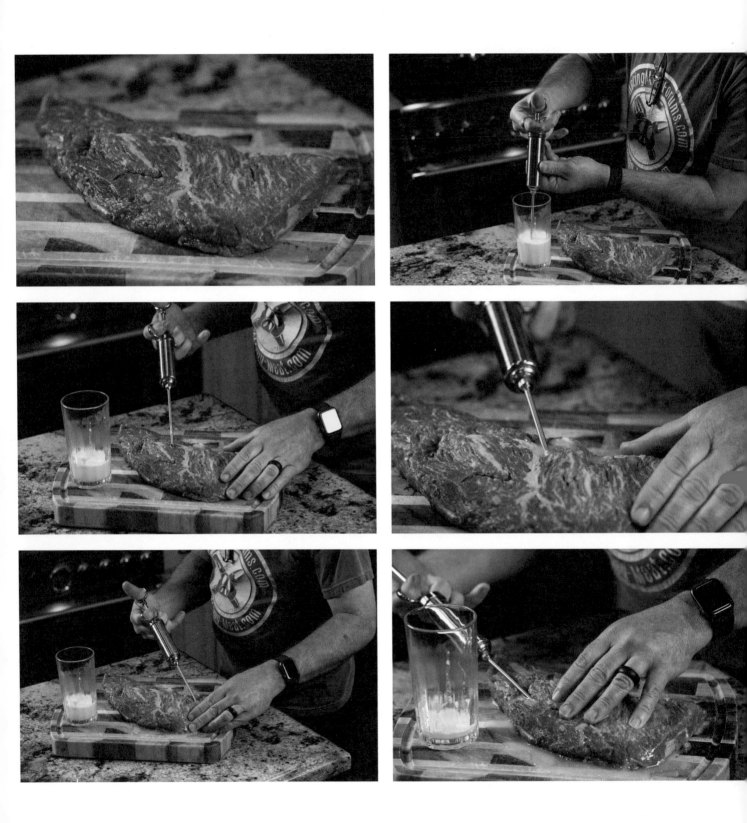

slowly pull out the plunger filling the injector barrel with the liquid.

The needle is then pressed into the meat at a 45-degree angle. With the needle in place inside of the meat, depress the plunger as you slowly pull back on the injector. You will be able to see the meat plumping up as it gets filled with the liquid. When you see the liquid start to back out of the injection hole, you can remove the injection needle from the meat.

This process is done about every two inches covering the entire surface of the meat until the meat is plumped up all over with the liquid. With a little practice you'll be able to insert the needle, depress the plunger and pull back on the injector simultaneously with one hand.

The sky is the limit where injection liquids are concerned but I will caution you to give a little thought to aesthetics when you are mixing them up and adding ingredients. For instance, injecting Worcestershire or other dark brown liquids into meat will cause streaking. Also make sure you are injecting liquid in the same direction as the grain of the meat to make the finished product look more appetizing when your guests cut into it.

Here is one of my favorite injection recipes:
- 1 stick (¼ pound) of melted butter, salted
- 1 cup of water
- 2 (heaping) tablespoons of low-salt barbecue rub (I use my original rub which can be purchased at thinbluefoods.com)

THE MEAT

The meat that you choose to cook is the star of the show. The sides, the bread, the dessert all help to make dinner better but the meat that you cook on the smoker or grill is the entrée and it's what people are going to remember when they leave your table.

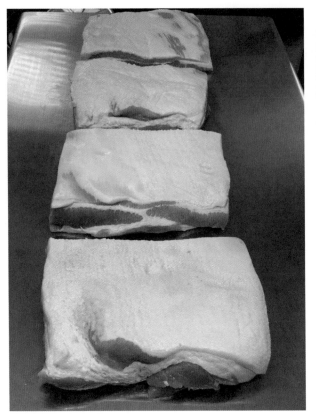 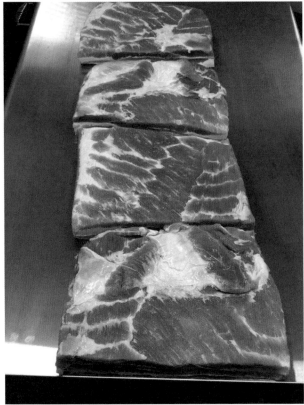

BASIC MEAT SAFETY

The Danger Zone

First and foremost, you need to know that there is a temperature range at which pathogens multiply at the greatest rate. This range is between 40°F and 140°F and as a general rule, whatever you are cooking needs to reach above 140°F in less than four hours in order for it to be safe to eat.

This 40°F to 140°F temperature range is appropriately called the "danger zone" and you will hear me and many others refer to it from time to time.

Food Pathogen Growth Rate

You also need to know that pathogens on cooked food double about every 20 minutes. From the time the food finishes cooking, you have about two hours at room temperature before the levels get high enough to cause sickness and/or death. This means the food needs to be in the fridge in less than two hours. Otherwise, it should be thrown away and not eaten. If the temperature is 90°F or higher, you only have one hour before the food is unsafe.

I know many of you probably have a story about how you've seen food sit on the table much longer than this and no one got sick. I remember having some friends when I was much younger who would fry chicken and leave it on the table for hours on end, even overnight, and throughout the evening—and even next morning—members of the family would come in and get a piece and continue eating it until it was all gone. I have no idea why all of them didn't die of food poisoning, but this kind of thing is very unsafe practice, and just because someone skated on death, it doesn't mean we should take unnecessary risks like that.

Cross Contamination

Make sure to keep cutting boards, utensils, anything that was used for raw meat, separate from cooked meat. I use a tablespoon of plain chlorine bleach in a gallon of water to sanitize cutting boards, cooking grates, temperature probes, and anything that touches raw meat.

After you handle raw meat, wash your hands with soap and warm water for at least 20 to 30 seconds. A good rule of thumb is to sing the happy birthday song or the ABC song twice to make sure you have washed your hands long enough to sanitize them.

In my opinion and according to many studies, good clean hands are more sanitary than wearing gloves. I do not wear gloves when I cook but you will see me wash my hands a hundred times during the preparation of a meal. The only time gloves are a great option is when you have a sore or cut on your hands. If this is the case, every time you would normally wash your hands, you remove your gloves, wash your hands, then put on a clean pair of gloves. Gloves give the impression of "sanitary" but they are far from it in most cases. I was in a restaurant a while back and a young lady answered the phone with her gloves on and then went right back to serving food with those same gloved hands. I walked out.

In the Store

I recommend shopping for your non-perishable items first and getting the meat, dairy, eggs, etc last thing, right before you're ready to check out. It might make sense to keep a cooler in your car or truck to keep such foods safe during the drive home–especially in summer!

Pay close attention to sell-by and use-by dates printed on food packaging. I don't care how good the meat looks or if it's priced to sell–if it's past the date, don't risk it.

Thawing Frozen Meat

I always recommend that people place meat in the fridge to thaw. This is without a doubt the safest method. Expect about five pounds of thawing per day.

In a pinch, you can thaw frozen meat in a waterproof container or bag in a clean sink full of cold tap water. Change the water every 30 minutes until the meat is thawed. Then cook immediately.

Storing Cooked Food

You generally have four days in the fridge after food is cooked to either eat it or freeze it. This is a good standard to live by.

The Smoker and Grill

Keep the grates clean. That black, burned-on food from three months ago is not flavor, it's food-borne illness just waiting to happen. I place all my smaller grates in the dishwasher every time I use them. My larger grates get cleaned by hand with hot water, soap, and elbow grease. I have had people give me a hard time about how clean I keep my smokers but I just feel like my family and friends are worth it. An ounce of prevention isn't really all that difficult and it does so much good.

WRAPPING IN FOIL VS PAPER

If you've been cooking for a while then it is likely that you have wrapped a brisket, pork butt, and maybe even ribs in heavy-duty aluminum foil. This is often to get you past that formidable stall

Resting meat after smoking will allow the juices to cool and redistribute throughout the meat.

that large roasts experience at about 160°F where the temperature just stops climbing for several hours. After a while, it will start to rise again but many get impatient and come to the forums or they email me asking what to do. Foil is truly the answer if you don't want to wait around for hours. In layman's terms, a stall is caused by the juices pooling on the outside of the meat where it starts to evaporate once the meat reaches a certain temperature. This cools the outside of the meat much like evaporating sweat cools your body—and it does take a while for the heat to overcome this phenomenon. Wrapping in foil at this point either stops the evaporation or helps the heat overcome it. At any rate, it speeds things up and for that reason, lots of brisket, pork butts, beef clods, etc. get wrapped in foil at around 160°F.

A secondary benefit to wrapping in foil is the tenderizing effect. When you wrap meat in foil, the liquid collects inside the foil instead of evaporating and it begins to steam inside the foil. This is essentially braising and is a form of cooking that steams meat to tenderness. The downside, if there is one, is that the crust gets soft and mushy instead of crisp and delicious just like most of us like it. We get around this sometimes by removing the meat from the foil about an hour before it's done to let the crust dry out and re-form.

RESTING

You will hear me and many others talking about "resting" the meat once it's finished cooking. This is very important for most things that we cook in the smoker.

During cooking the juices that are in the meat get very hot and travel from the center of the meat out to the edges. The juices are also under a lot of pressure and even more so if the meat is cooked to a very high temperature as you would brisket, pork butt or chicken.

By allowing the meat to rest for a few minutes after removing it from the smoker, the juices cool down and redistribute throughout the meat. In this way, when you do cut into it, more of the juice stays inside and less of it ends up on the cutting board.

I like to place a piece of foil over the meat loosely, like a tent, so it can cool down gradually rather than quickly. This seems to give the best end result.

As a general rule, the larger the piece of meat, the longer it will need to rest before cutting into it. Resting times usually range between 10 minutes and 30 minutes. But any resting is better than nothing, so if you like to rest a brisket for 30 minutes but everyone is sitting there starving, then 15 minutes is a good alternative.

SPECIAL TIPS ON MAKING SLICED BREAKFAST BACON

"Bacon" is such a wonderful word and every time I hear it, my salivary glands go into full production. Just now as I write this I think about our family tradition of pancakes with real maple syrup and neat little piles of bacon that we cook up every Saturday morning. We've done this since our kids were young. But today it includes a son-in-law, our two grandkids and several other relatives that just happen to be in the neighborhood . . . They all know they're welcome and I always make enough pancakes and bacon to feed a small army.

Of course I'm referring to the "streaky" bacon that we Americans make from pork belly and it's just something that many of us go crazy over. We eat it plain, we wrap things with it, we add it to our vegetables to make them taste better, and if you go to the local fair you might find it deep-fried.

If you really knew how easy it was to make, you'd probably never purchase it from the store. Well, lucky you. While this isn't a recipe book per se, I just couldn't resist showing you how it's done. I'm going to show you just how simple it is to make bacon at home and yes, it takes a little time but most of this time consists of just waiting on it to finish soaking in the brine, which takes about 10 days.

Let's start off by explaining that what we call bacon here in the United States is quite a bit different than what it's called in other places. Not to confound things but bacon is also made in different ways using different parts of the pig depending on where you are from.

For instance, Canadian (back) bacon is all the rage with our Canadian friends. When they say "bacon" that's back bacon made from the loin. I'm not going to argue the point as to which is better since that's quite subjective and probably depends on which side of the border you were raised on. But I can tell you that I never met bacon I didn't like.

ANTHONY'S
PINK CURING SALT #1
PREMIUM PRAGUE POWDER
MADE IN USA

BATCH TESTED AND VERIFIED
GLUTEN FREE

Net wt 2 lb (90

SOURCING CURING SALT AND PORK BELLY

The first thing you have to do if you decide you want to make some American style "streaky" bacon is to source the curing salt, also called pink salt, also called curing salt #1, also called insta-cure #1. You will know it's the right one when you read the ingredients and it says 6.25% sodium nitrite.

I usually order this from Amazon in a one- or two-pound package and it lasts me a while. You can purchase the same stuff I use at https://www.smoking-meat.com/pink-salt or you can go to Amazon and just do a search for curing salt #1 and make sure the percentage of sodium nitrite is correct.

The next thing you have to find is some pork belly. I often get mine from Costco –and it's not only high quality but they already have the rind or outer skin removed which saves me a little time. You might also be able to find it at a local meat market or by asking the guy behind the meat counter at your local grocery store.

I highly recommend purchasing the best quality you can afford and go from there.

With curing salt #1 and an 8-10 lb pork belly or a couple of them if you are really ambitious, you've done the hard part–and now it's time to make some bacon.

Let's make up a gallon of brine and that'll be about the right amount for one pork belly.

POPS CURING BRINE

This brine comes from a man at smokingmeatforums.com who knows his bacon well–his family has been in the meat business for a very long time. He has so kindly shared his brine with me and others and he has given me special permission to share it with you as well as in this book.

Please note that I have used what he calls his low-sodium version and I have modified that to include Morton's coarse kosher salt instead of table salt. The salt level in this recipe was "in the pocket" and at least 10 other people told me it was perfectly salted.

Having said that, everyone's salt tolerance is different and later I will show you how to test and reduce the salt level if needed after curing the pork belly and just before smoking it.

Ingredients

1 gallon cold, clean water

1 ounce curing salt #1 (this is equivalent to a heaping tablespoon)

¾ cup Morton's coarse kosher salt

½ cup white granulated sugar

½ cup brown sugar (I use dark but light will work)

Instructions

Pour the water into a large stock pot or something that holds at least 6 quarts.

Add the curing salt, Morton's coarse kosher salt, white, and brown sugar into the water and stir for about two minutes or until the brine becomes a clear amber color and all ingredients are dissolved into the water.

TIP: I recommend making the brine about a day ahead of time then place it into the fridge to get cold.

NOTE: I do not recommend leaving out the sugars unless it is absolutely necessary as this is a part of the flavor profile. But if you are in a situation where sugar is not an option, you can safely omit the sugars as they are for flavor only.

CURING THE PORK BELLY

To prepare and cure the pork belly, I recommend first cutting it in half to give you two easy-to-manage pieces.

Once in two pieces, you'll want to remove the thick skin if it hasn't already been removed. This is a job for a very sharp knife and a willingness to learn.

Just start cutting under the thick skin while pulling up on it with your free hand. Continue to pull upward on the skin as you move the knife between the skin and the thick layer of fat.

There's not really a right or wrong way to do this. Remember, though, that you'll get better at this the more you do it.

Once the skin or "rind" is removed, you can discard it or save it for making homemade pork rinds. This is not something we'll cover here but Youtube and other online sources will be your friend if you want to meddle with this a little bit.

Place the two halves of the now-skinless pork belly into your brining container.

I use a 9-liter Tupperware container from the "W" mart and it is about as near perfect as you will find for a whole pork belly cut in half.

Pour the brine over the pork belly to cover. More than likely your pork belly will try to float to the top. This is not good. We want everything submerged. Fix this problem by filling a quart-sized zip-top bag with water, zipping it closed, and then placing that on top of the floating meat.

When you place the lid on the container, the bag of water will force the meat below the brine.

Put the container(s) of brining pork bellies into the fridge and set your timer for 10 days. I wrote the start date and projected finish date on my fridge using a wet erase marker. My brain cannot be trusted to remember things like this so I have learned to write it down where it's easy to see.

Ten days later, and with great anticipation, remove the brining container from the fridge, lay one of the pork belly halves on a cutting board, and with a very sharp knife cut off a small strip of the cured meat.

Fry it up in a skillet and taste test it to make sure it's not too salty.

IF IT'S TOO SALTY: Discard the brine and fill the brining container with cold, clean water. Place the pork belly halves into the water and soak them for about two hours in the fridge. Test it again and repeat as many times as necessary using fresh, clean, cold water each time until enough of the salt has leached out.

Using the recipe above, the salt level was perfect for me and my family and no soaking was required. Nevertheless, this is a fairly painless way to make sure the saltiness is perfect before you smoke it and slice it.

IF IT'S NOT TOO SALTY AND TASTES JUST RIGHT: Discard the brine and rinse the pork belly halves under cold water to remove any residual salt from the outside of the meat.

Pat the pork belly as dry as you can with paper towels, then place it on racks uncovered and back into the fridge to dry. It's important that you allow the meat to form a pellicle or a very dry tackiness on the outside. This helps the smoke to adhere to the meat and will make a much better-tasting bacon.

I usually let the bacon dry for a full 24-hour period for best results, but if you are short on time or impatient for bacon, 4-6 hours will work just fine.

Once the pork belly is dry and feels tacky to the touch, it's time to smoke this stuff and make it taste amazing.

SMOKING THE PORK BELLY

When smoking bacon, you are looking to smoke it at a fairly low temperature for a number of hours. This is to give it a lot of good, natural smoke flavor and to bring it up to about 146°F internal temperature.

When you get done with this bacon, it will no longer be raw and will be ready to throw into a skillet for crisping up.

The USDA says that pork, other than ground pork, is safe to eat once it reaches 145°F plus a three-minute rest. If you cook pork belly, and all pork cuts and roasts for that matter, to 146°F, this ensures you have met those requirements and the pork is safe to serve to your guests.

Set-up your smoker for somewhere between 160-180°F if possible but 200°F is okay if that's as low as your smoker will go. Use indirect heat; and if your smoker uses a water pan, fill it up.

Once the smoker is ready to go, place the pork belly directly on the smoker grate and let it smoke away.

Be sure to use a thermometer to monitor the temperature of the meat while it cooks since it needs to be pulled out just as soon as it hits 146°F.

I used a pellet smoker for the bacon in these pictures and with the controls set to "Low Smoke," it took about seven hours for the meat to reach temperature. The higher your temperature, the quicker it will reach temperature.

I like to opt for a lower temperature and longer time so it has more time in the smoke–but that is something you can decide for yourself.

NOTE: Yes, you can make the bacon in an oven if you get caught short somewhere without a smoker–but it won't taste smoky. I don't recommend liquid smoke as I don't like it and don't use it but if you want to add some to the brine, it's your bacon and you can add a couple of teaspoons per gallon of brine if you so desire.

SLICE AND BAG FOR STORAGE

When the bacon gets done smoking and has reached an internal temperature of 146°F you should remove it from the heat right away and set it aside to cool down.

Go ahead and slice off a strip or two to test, you know you can't resist, then place the rest of it in the fridge so it can get really cold. There are (two) reasons for letting it cool:

• Cold bacon slices better
• The smoke seems to settle into the meat more and the flavor gets better after a few hours or a full day in the fridge.

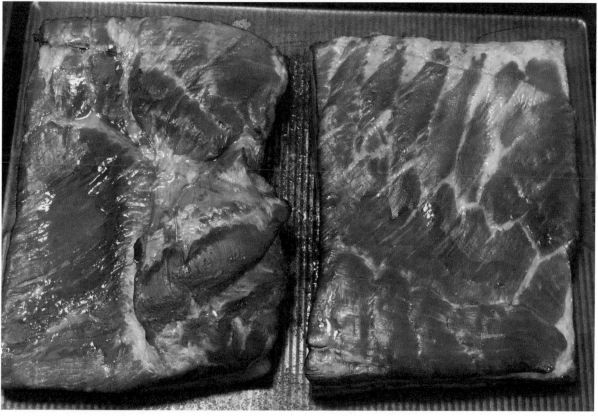

I usually wait a full day before slicing but that's almost unbearable so I put a chain and padlock on my fridge and hide the key from myself. You'll see what I mean when you smell this homemade stuff!

The next day has arrived so you'll want a very sharp knife and lots of patience or a decent slicer. My slicer is not expensive and though it's not perfect, it does a pretty good job of getting the work done.

Keep the bacon cold for as long as you can—hey, you can even place it in the freezer for an hour or two if you need to before slicing it.

Decide on a thickness and slice away until you have a beautiful pile of sliced bacon before you. Take a break once in a while to admire your handiwork and then get right back after it.

I don't own a vacuum sealer but that would be a very nice investment if you have the funds. I do just fine putting the bacon a pound at a time into gallon-sized zip-top bags. I have found that this is easier if you stack it onto heavy-duty paper plates first to give it some rigidity.

Put the bagged bacon right back into the fridge as quickly as you can. If you have some that you don't plan to use or give away in the next week or so, place it in the freezer for up to three months of storage.

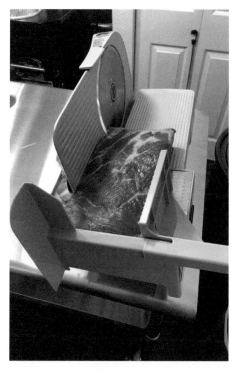

EXTRAS

This is a collected list of general cooking terms I feel every cook should know, even if you aren't classically trained:

AL DENTE: Italian term meaning pasta cooked until tender but still firm to the bite.

AU JUS: French term meaning served in natural meat juices.

BAKE: To cook foods in the oven at a temperature specified in recipe.

BASTE: To spread, brush or spoon water, melted fat or other liquid, such as chicken broth, over food to keep the surface moist and add flavor.

BEAT: To make a mixture smooth or to introduce air by using a brisk, regular revolving motion that lifts the mixture over and over.

BLANCH: To boil in water for a short time and then plunge into cold water, or to pour boiling water over food, then drain it almost immediately. Often used to preserve color in vegetables or to loosen the skin of tomatoes.

BLEND: To combine two or more ingredients by mixing thoroughly.

BOIL: To cook in boiling water or other liquid. Liquid is at a "boil" when large bubbles rise continuously to the top.

BONE (AS A VERB): To remove bones from meat, poultry or fish.

BRAISE: To brown in fat, then cook covered on top of the stove or in the oven with some added liquid.

BREAD (AS A VERB): To roll or coat with bread crumbs, dry cereal or cracker crumbs.

BROIL: To cook by direct heat.

BRUSH: To spread or brush with melted fat or other liquid to coat.

BUTTERFLY (AS A VERB): To cut a piece of meat, fish or poultry in half horizontally, leaving one side attached. This is sometimes called spatch-cocking when referring to butterflied poultry.

CHILL: To cool in the refrigerator.

CHOP: To cut into small pieces with a sharp knife.

COAT THE SPOON: To cook until mixture sticks to the metal stirring spoon in a thin layer.

CREAM (AS A VERB): To beat one or more foods until mixture is soft and creamy or fluffy. Usually a step at the beginning of baking recipes.

CUBE (AS A VERB): To cut into small squares of equal (or semi-equal) size.

CUT IN SHORTENING: To combine shortening (or any other solid fat) with flour and other dry ingredients by chopping it into mixture with a pastry cutter, or two knives or spatulas.

DICE: To cut into small cubes. Size may be specified in recipe, such as "¼-inch dice" or "½-inch dice."

DOT: To scatter small pieces of butter or other fat over food before cooking.

DREDGE: To coat or sprinkle lightly with flour, sugar, etc., until food is well-covered.

DUST: To sprinkle food lightly with a dry ingredient, such as paprika.

FOLD: To combine by using two motions: (1) cutting vertically through the mixture and (2) turning over and over by sliding the implement across the bottom of the mixing bowl with each turn of the bowl. Usually accomplished with a spatula, and usually used to incorporate light mixtures, such as egg whites, into other mixtures, such as cake batter.

GARNISH: To decorate foods, usually with other foods.

GLAZE: To brush or pour a shiny coating over foods.

GRATE: To cut food into very fine particles by rubbing on a grater. Spray a grater with non-stick spray to help in cleanup.

GREASE: To rub lightly with shortening or butter. Often, you can squirt pans with non-stick spray instead.

GRIND: To cut food into tiny particles by pushing through a food grinder, or by crushing with a mortar and pestle. Also can be accomplished in a food processor.

KNEAD: To repeatedly fold, turn and press down on dough with the hands until it becomes smooth and elastic. One of the most rewarding physical tasks in cooking.

MARINATE: To let food stand in a liquid mixture. Refrigerate, covered, if marinating more than two hours.

MINCE: To cut or chop into very small pieces.

MIX: To combine ingredients in any way that evenly distributes them.

PARBOIL: To cook in a skillet kept dry by pouring off accumulated fat. Usually, fattier meats are parboiled.

PAN-FRY: To cook in a small amount of fat in a skillet. Usually, leaner meats are pan-fried.

PEEL: To strip off the outside covering.

POACH: To cook in water, broth or other liquid that is just below the boiling point.

PREHEAT: To heat oven to desired temperature before putting food in oven. Preheat for 20 minutes when baking for a proper rise.

PUNCH DOWN: To strike down risen dough with the fist to allow gas to escape.

ROAST: To cook by dry heat in oven.

SAUTE: To cook briskly in a small amount of fat, usually in a skillet on top of the stove. Same thing as pan-fry.

SCALD: To heat milk to just below the boiling point. Small bubbles will appear around the edges when scalded.

SEAR: To brown surfaces quickly over high heat, usually in a hot skillet. Often an instruction at the beginning of meat preparation.

SHRED: To tear into fine pieces with a knife or sharp instruments.

SIFT: To put dry ingredients through a sieve or sifter, to lighten and/or incorporate them, or to remove large pieces.

SIMMER: To cook in liquid at a low temperature. Be sure the liquid does not boil.

SLIVER: To slice into long, thin strips.

SOFT PEAKS: To beat egg whites or whipping cream until peaks are formed. When beaters are lifted, the tips of peaks will curl over.

STEAM (VERB FORM): To cook, covered, over a small amount of boiling liquid so the steam formed in the pan does the cooking.

STEEP: Let stand in hot liquid to extract flavor, as in tea, or to hydrate dried vegetables or fruits.

STEW: To cook slowly in liquid.

STIR: To mix foods with a circular motion for the purpose of blending or obtaining uniform consistency.

THIN: To dilute by adding liquid.

TOSS: To lightly blend ingredients by lifting them and letting them fall back in the bowl.

ZEST: The colored part of citrus rind used as a flavoring.

INDEX